"Endearing, raw, and honest. A heartfelt contribution to the growing literature on openly gay lives of fruitful obedience in the traditional churches."
Eve Tushnet, author of *Gay and Catholic*

"Simply fabulous. Wonderfully honest. Superbly written. Deeply inspiring in its powerful portrayal of one person's struggle to choose Jesus above all. I learned so much from this fantastic story of Greg's both agonizing and exhilarating journey in faith. This is a book every Christian—especially heterosexual evangelicals—must read if we are to learn to love our LGBTQ neighbors, friends, and Christian brothers and sisters the way Jesus does."
Ronald J. Sider, Palmer Seminary at Eastern University

"To say this book is important is a painful understatement. It is the candid, moving, intensely personal story of a gay young man who wants to live his life under the authority of King Jesus and who refuses to accept the comforting answers proffered by different parts of the culture. Superbly written, this book stands athwart the shibboleths of our day and reminds us what submission to King Jesus looks like, what it feels like. This book needs to be thoughtfully read by straight people and by gay people, by unbelievers and by Christians. It is not to be read with a condescending smirk, but with humility."
D. A. Carson, president, The Gospel Coalition, research professor of New Testament, Trinity Evangelical Divinity School

"Before we can speak, we must listen. Especially to those who have been marginalized, pushed aside, and undervalued. This book serves as an opportunity to do just that. To hear from a man who knows and loves Jesus and wrestles honestly with himself and God. Listen to him. Hear his story. Enter into another perspective, a narrative that is often untold."
Andy Mineo, hip-hop artist

"Greg has written a book that is a delight to read because of both the beauty of his writing and his main message: that our good God made no mistakes in either making him the way that he is or asking him to live life the way that he is."
Ed Shaw, author of *Same-Sex Attraction and the Church*

"I found Greg's poignant autobiography not just to be intellectually and theologically honest, but also to be a poetic and wonderfully human book. *Single, Gay, Christian* is nourishment for the soul of anyone who seeks to love Jesus in our times. It captured my heart as I am sure it will yours. I loved it!"
Debra Hirsch, author of *Redeeming Sex*

"Greg Coles has poured himself out beautifully in this transparent account of his life with Christ as a young gay man. He asks whether the Bible leaves room for monogamous same-sex relationships and agonizes over how the church will treat singleness and sexual minorities. His answers are not easy. Especially for him. If you want to be inspired by one man's deep and unfailing love of Jesus, read this book. If you or someone you love is a follower of Jesus who happens to be gay, this is a must-read."

Carolyn Carney, assistant regional director of spiritual formation and prayer, InterVarsity Christian Fellowship

"I couldn't put it down. The blend of experience, wisdom, and beautiful prose grabbed hold of my heart and sent me on an adventure. Thank you, Greg, for challenging so much of what I thought I knew about the topic (and people!) of faith and sexuality. I cannot more highly recommend this book."

Preston Sprinkle, president of The Center for Faith, Sexuality & Gender, author of *People to Be Loved*

SINGLE GAY CHRISTIAN

A PERSONAL JOURNEY OF FAITH AND SEXUAL IDENTITY

GREGORY COLES
FOREWORD BY WESLEY HILL

IVP Books

An imprint of InterVarsity Press
Downers Grove, Illinois

InterVarsity Press
P.O. Box 1400, Downers Grove, IL 60515-1426
ivpress.com
email@ivpress.com

InterVarsity Press® is the book-publishing division of InterVarsity Christian Fellowship/USA®, a movement of students and faculty active on campus at hundreds of universities, colleges, and schools of nursing in the United States of America, and a member movement of the International Fellowship of Evangelical Students. For information about local and regional activities, visit intervarsity.org.

All Scripture quotations, unless otherwise indicated, are taken from THE HOLY BIBLE, NEW INTERNATIONAL VERSION®, NIV® Copyright © 1973, 1978, 1984, 2011 by Biblica, Inc.™ Used by permission. All rights reserved worldwide.

This book is published in association with Nappaland Literary Agency, an independent agency dedicated to publishing works that are: Authentic. Relevant. Eternal. Visit us on the web at nappalandliterary.com.

While any stories in this book are true, some names and identifying information may have been changed to protect the privacy of individuals.

Cover design: Cindy Kiple
Interior design: Daniel van Loon

ISBN 978-0-8308-4512-5 (print)
ISBN 978-0-8308-9093-4 (digital)

Printed in the United States of America ♾

 As a member of the Green Press Initiative, InterVarsity Press is committed to protecting the environment and to the responsible use of natural resources. To learn more, visit greenpressinitiative.org.

Library of Congress Cataloging-in-Publication Data

Names: Coles, Gregory, 1990- author.
Title: Single, gay, Christian : a personal journey of faith and sexual
*   identity / Gregory Coles ; foreword by Wesley Hill.*
Description: Downers Grove : InterVarsity Press, 2017.
Identifiers: LCCN 2017019249 (print) | LCCN 2017024358 (ebook) | ISBN
*   9780830890934 (eBook) | ISBN 9780830845125 (pbk. : alk. paper)*
Subjects: LCSH: Coles, Gregory, 1990- | Gays—Religious life. | Christian
*   biography. | Gays—Biography. | Homosexuality—Religious*
*   aspects—Christianity.*
Classification: LCC BV4596.G38 (ebook) | LCC BV4596.G38 C65 2017 (print) |
*   DDC 248.8/408664—dc23*
LC record available at https://lccn.loc.gov/2017019249

P   21   20   19   18   17   16   15   14   13   12   11   10   9   8   7   6   5   4   3   2   1

Y   35   34   33   32   31   30   29   28   27   26   25   24   23   22   21   20   19   18   17

For Aaron and Amy,

through whose eyes I learned to see myself
as more than a divine typo.

CONTENTS

FOREWORD

WESLEY HILL

TEN YEARS AGO—ONLY TEN SHORT YEARS AGO—it was impossible to find a book like this. I know because I tried.

For what felt like an agonizing length of time, I searched far and wide for a book like the one you now hold in your hands.

A book in which an author talked frankly about being gay, rather than "ex-gay" or just "struggling with same-sex attraction."

A book in which an author described why and how one might choose to be gay *and single*, rather than "gay affirming" or "theologically progressive" or "revisionist."

A book in which an author wrestled honestly with being gay, single, *and Christian*—rather than "formerly Christian" or merely "spiritual but not religious."

A book in which an author didn't just talk about having formerly lived a "homosexual lifestyle" (as if there were only one!) but one in which he narrated an *ongoing* experience of same-sex desire and all that goes along with that.

A book in which an author didn't just lay out the biblical case for "traditional Christian marriage" but also grappled with the dawning realization that, however much he might want such a marriage for himself, it didn't seem likely to be in his future.

A book in which an author told a story about what it *felt* like to be seeking to live in that awkward in-between space that Greg Coles's title names with such beguiling simplicity: single, gay, Christian.

I ended up trying to write such a book myself, because my own life, like Greg's, is one of ongoing same-sex desire, voluntary singleness, and committed Christian faith. But I quickly learned, as my book found its way into the hands of many different readers, that not everyone who shares my circumstances—not everyone who is single, gay, and Christian—experiences those circumstances in the same way or asks exactly the same questions or cherishes the same consolations.

It seems like an obvious point now, but it took me a while to feel its weight: not only did the Christian world need one book about being single, gay, and Christian, it needed *dozens* of books about it—because there is no one way of living that complicated, multifaceted story.

And that's why I am grateful for Greg Coles's searingly honest, beautifully written book. I'm grateful for it because it offers exactly the sort of comfort and challenge I needed when I was just beginning to navigate life as a self-described gay Christian. But I'm especially grateful for it because Greg's book will offer the sort of hope and insight that *other* gay Christians might not be able to find in my testimony. I'm grateful for it because it offers one more snapshot of what a faithful gay Christian life might look like, and God knows we need as many such snapshots as we can get.

There are so many of us, from such varied cultures, races, Christian denominations, and family backgrounds, who have come out as gay and Christian in recent years. And each of us is seeking to learn, in our own way, how to flourish as we embrace intentional Christian singleness. We need stories like Greg's to remind us that there are as many ways to flourish in those circumstances as there are Christians who embrace them.

One of the early church fathers wrote wisely, "Any theory divorced from living examples . . . is like an unbreathing statue." That plural—*examples*—is vital. That's why I'm so glad for Greg's book: it offers one more example, one more story, one more urgent reminder that no one's story is interchangeable with or reducible to anyone else's. It's a timely, evocative reminder that each single, gay, Christian life is equally unique and precious.

PRELUDE

PROMISES

LET'S MAKE A DEAL, YOU AND ME. Let's make promises to each other.

I promise to tell you my story. The whole story. I'll tell you about a boy in love with Jesus who, at the fateful onset of puberty, realized his sexual attractions were persistently and exclusively for other guys. I'll tell you how I lay on my bed in the middle of the night and whispered to myself the words I've whispered a thousand times since:

"I'm gay."

I'll tell you how I cried and prayed and begged God to make me straight, or else to make me believe that the Bible left room for monogamous same-sex relationships. I'll tell you how God kept refusing to do either one, how he kept pointing me back to the cross of Christ. How I followed my Savior in costly obedience and became a mythical creature, a thing that wasn't supposed to exist: a single gay Christian.

I'll show you the world through my eyes: The books on Christian masculinity that never seemed to be about me. The churches that treated my singleness like an acne problem that could be cleared up with a few weeks' treatment. The sincere Christians who called it "love" when they talked about people like me with revulsion in their voices.

I'll tell you what it's like to belong nowhere. To know that much of my Christian family will forever consider me unnatural, dangerous, because of something that feels as involuntary as my eye color. And to know that much of the LGBTQ community that shares my experience as a sexual minority will disagree with the way I've chosen to interpret the call of Jesus, believing I've bought into a tragic, archaic ritual of self-hatred.

Self-hatred. I'll tell you about that too. I'll tell you how hard it is some days to look in the mirror and believe that God could have possibly said over me, as he did over all creation, "It is good."

But I promise my story won't all be sadness and loneliness and struggle. I'll tell you good things too, hopeful things, funny things, like the time I accidentally came out to my best friend during his bachelor party. I'll tell you what it felt like the first time someone looked me in the eyes and said, "You are not a mistake." I'll tell you that joy and sorrow are not opposites, that my life has never been more beautiful than when it was most brokenhearted.

If you'll listen, I promise I'll tell you everything, and you can decide for yourself what you want to believe about me.

All you have to promise in return is that you'll wait a little while before you reach your verdict about me. Wait until you've heard everything. Wait until you know me. And then, well . . .

Then the rest is up to you.

1

REVELATION

I THOUGHT A LOT ABOUT DEATH AS A CHILD. It wasn't that I was morbid—quite the opposite. I was excited for heaven. I longed for it with a simple, childish logic, the way I longed for weekends and birthdays. Heaven seemed more real, more imminent, more permanent than any other promise I knew.

It probably didn't hurt that I was living at the time in Indonesia, a Muslim-majority nation in the throes of political upheaval. The thirty-one-year regime of president/dictator Suharto was on its deathbed during the mid-1990s, anticipating Indonesia's first democratic election in 1999. In 1996 a political scuffle in the capital city, Jakarta, left more than a hundred dead or injured on a day now remembered as *Sabtu Kelabu* (Gray Saturday).

My home city of Bandung was a four-hour drive from the capital, but it wasn't exempt from the violence. Rumored deaths and riots in the street weren't uncommon. One day my brothers went out to play basketball and came home hours later than they should have, explaining that they had gotten trapped in the middle of a standoff between rioters and police, hiding behind a car that had its front window shattered by a rock. There were months I kept a shelf in my closet packed for quick travel, in case we needed to evacuate the country with twenty-four hours' notice or less.

I grew up hearing my parents say that the safest place in the world was the place God wanted you to be. By this logic, our life in Indonesia was safe—or at least as safe as anywhere could be. And so we stayed put, an English teacher from New York and his homeschooling wife and four kids who had gotten used to living in a country built on eggshells.

The world was dangerous, and heaven was glorious. These were the two things I knew with certainty by the age of seven. And so it felt like the most natural thing in the world, when my dad brought me a bedtime sip of water in a teal plastic cup one night, to ask how I could make sure I was going to heaven.

In retrospect, I had a very utilitarian view of God. But for my seven-year-old self, it was enough. As I closed my eyes extra tight and clenched my hands together and promised to surrender my whole life to Jesus, the exchange felt almost too easy, like I'd traded a safety pin for a Stradivarius. I promised God something I already knew was out of my control, and he, in return, promised me everything.

My promise never changed, and neither did his. But somehow, as the years went by, things got more complicated.

■ ◼ ■

Puberty came in the way a car crash comes, with a screech of tires: enough warning to scare the crap out of me, but not enough to save me from the wreckage. I had read about it in books, heard murmurs of it at youth group, seen it beginning to happen to my friends. As I understood it, puberty turned boys into sex-crazed animals. It made them throw out the logic of Jesus and love and family so they could look at pictures of naked girls.

One day I walked in on a friend a few years older than me looking at online pornography. When he saw me, his face became a mask of shame and terror. He tried to close the web browser, accidentally making an obscene picture his desktop background.

"I'm sorry," he said, standing and trying to cover the screen with his scrawny chest. "Don't look at this."

Dutifully, I went and sat on a stack of pillows in the corner, where I couldn't see the face of the computer monitor.

"I'm sorry," he said again, sitting down and clicking furiously, trying to erase the evidence of what he had done. "This stuff is bad. It's wrong. I'm trying not to look at it anymore. I don't want to be looking at it."

"Okay," I said, staring at him blankly.

"When you get older," he said, "you'll understand."

I thought of the scantily clad woman on his computer screen. The image repulsed me. I didn't want to understand.

Some nights in the youth group at my English-speaking Indonesian church, they would split us up, the boys and the girls, which inevitably meant we were going to talk about sex. The male leaders, their faces somber, would wrangle the middle-school boys and tell us about what we were all going through, the way we wanted to look at girls, the way we shouldn't look at girls. It was everyone's struggle, they said, and that made it okay to be honest with each other. We could confess our shameful thoughts and pray together in godly, manly sorts of ways.

Everyone else seemed to be nodding along with these talks, so I nodded along too and kept my mouth shut. If we broke up into small groups and I had to speak, I used vague words like *struggle* and *lust*, words that were really just middle-school code for masturbation. As far as I could tell, I had the part about girls already figured out. I had no problem looking just at a girl's face or keeping her fully clothed in my mind. I already thought of girls as friends, sisters in Christ, God's holy creations.

So while everyone else was in a skirmish for purity, learning what it meant to save themselves for marriage and honor God as sexual beings, I was sitting on the sidelines. Confused. Bracing myself for a sledgehammer blow that never seemed to come.

Maybe, I thought, this was God's way of blessing me, his way of rewarding me for my faithfulness. He was sparing me from the gross obsession with naked women that every other boy I knew had been cursed with. Some days I almost threw out my elbow patting myself on the back. In the race to purity, I was winning.

Or so I thought.

■ ▣ ■

While I was busy steeling myself against the sexual desires everyone told me were coming, other desires were creeping in unnoticed. At first I thought it was just curiosity. What did other guys look like naked? Did they look like me? What would they think of seeing me naked? What would it be like to be naked with another guy?

If these were sexual questions, lustful questions, I had no way of knowing. No one had ever warned me about them. I knew same-sex changing rooms existed, though I'd never been inside one. I'd heard people talk about skinny-dipping in ponds with friends when no one had a bathing suit. The stories seemed innocent, innocuous. Why were my questions any different?

Slowly, carefully, without admitting to myself what I was doing, I began seeking out images of naked men and stories that involved nudity. Greek and Roman myths, I discovered, were a treasure trove of nude or almost nude illustrations. Encyclopedias had pictures of everything, if you knew where to look. (All in the name of

education, of course.) *Huckleberry Finn* had a few passing references to nudity, and I read those sentences over and over, pretending I was with Huck, pretending I *was* Huck.

The pictures and thoughts gave me a tingly feeling, excited, ravenous. I felt instinctively that it was a secret feeling, something I
needed to keep to myself, and that made me wonder if it was wrong.
But in my limited vocabulary, what I was doing and thinking and
feeling had nothing to do with sex.

If there were no girls involved, it couldn't be sexual—could it?

It was months before I finally put the pieces together. Masturbation, I knew, was how most guys my age expressed their sexual
desires for women, and now more and more of my searches for
male nudity were ending the same way. I hadn't escaped the
struggle my friends were having. I had switched it, exchanged one
repulsive urge for another.

But it didn't make sense. It wasn't the way puberty was supposed
to happen.

So I scoured the books on puberty again. I googled web articles.
(Actually, this was before the reign of Google had begun. I used an
obscure search engine named Metacrawler, with hopes that no one
else in my family would use it on our family computer and notice
my incriminating search history.) And that was when I noticed for
the first time the word that would change my life:

Gay.

I was gay.

I would lie on the bottom bunk of the bunkbed I shared with
one of my brothers, staring up at the warped wooden slats and the
underside of his mattress. I would kick off my covers, sweating in
the tropical heat, and whisper just loud enough for the sound to
reach back to my own ears:

"I'm gay. I'm gay. I'm gay."

If I had been reserved and private about my sexuality before, this revelation sealed my lips even tighter. I knew next to nothing about homosexuality, but I knew it was a topic reserved for hushed tones and sorrowful eyes. It wasn't something nice Christian boys like me talked about, not something they should need or want to understand.

The only person I told, in seventh grade or so, was my brother, and then only because he asked me such a pointed question about my struggle with lust that there was no way of answering him without either blatantly lying or telling the impossible truth. We were the only ones in the house that day, and he had just come home in the middle of a torrential Indonesian rainstorm, his clothes and shoes and hair sopping wet.

I don't remember how we ended up on the topic of sexual purity, but I remember his question, and the way my heart stopped when he asked it.

I looked him in the eyes, my hands and chin trembling, and called him by my favorite of his nicknames. "I think I'm gay," I said.

For a minute he didn't say anything. Then he said, "No you're not. You're not gay."

I didn't have an answer. He went on.

Homosexuality, he said, was something fluid, an open door you didn't have to walk through. It was an idea your adolescent mind played with when it was flooded with sexual tension, when you were so aroused you could have lusted after a mop bucket. "Just because you have those thoughts," he said, "it doesn't make you gay. You're just like the rest of us."

"Okay," I said, and I wanted so badly to believe him.

The next time I saw a picture of a woman in a tight-fitting bathing suit, I tried hard to admire her. Tried to feel what I was supposed to feel. Maybe, I thought, if I believed a little more, if I tried a little harder, I would finally unlock my true sexual self.

I might as well have been staring at an office supplies poster. I felt nothing.

"How's it going?" my brother asked a few weeks later, checking in on me. "With . . . you know . . . *that*?"

"I don't know," I said. "I think maybe it's getting better. Yes, it's definitely getting a little better."

"Good," he said. And for years we didn't talk about it again. Looking back, I can't remember if he never brought it up or if I changed the subject every time he did.

■ ◙ ■

It wasn't until much later that I realized how unfair it had been of me to dump on a high school sophomore the darkest secret I knew, demand his silence, and then expect his answer to be the gospel truth. He tried, because he loved me. But there was no way he could have understood me when I didn't even understand myself.

Perhaps my brother had been wrong—and yet, I thought, he was right, wasn't he? I couldn't be gay. Because being gay was supposed to be a choice, a lifestyle, a sin. And I hadn't chosen anything, not that I remembered. I hadn't meant to sin. Was it possible to sin just by existing? Was it possible to inadvertently defy God with every breath you breathed?

Most of the books and articles I read mentioned people like me as an afterthought, a footnote, three sentences buried in the middle of chapter five. "If you're gay," they said, "it's because of your rebellion against God." "If you're gay, it's because you had a distant father and an overbearing mother." "If you're gay, you were probably abused as a child." "If you're gay, you obviously lack close male friendships."

Worst of all was when they said, "If you're afraid you might be gay, don't worry about it. It's extremely rare. It can't possibly happen to you."

Nothing fit. I wasn't in rebellion against God, except in the sense that any sinner caught in the grip of grace might be. I loved God. I had two loving parents, three loving older siblings, a host of dear friends both male and female, and (national upheaval aside) a remarkably untroubled childhood. I couldn't read into my past some trauma that hadn't happened.

And yet here I was. An enigma. An impossibility. A twisted upside-down miracle.

I prayed for God to turn the miracle right side up. I begged him to make me straight. One night when my brother wasn't home, I lay facedown on the floor of our shared bedroom and stretched out my arms, imagining I was Isaac waiting on the altar, ready to give his life at God's command. "Please," I said. "I'm all yours. Change me. Fix me. Make me clean."

When I finally stood up, my neck was stiff, and my face and the tile floor were both damp with tears. I felt spent, empty, at peace. And I was just as gay as ever.

* ■ *

After that night, I thought about death even more than usual. I wanted to die. Not suicide—I was too happy, even in the middle of my anguish, for that. But I wanted God to take me home. I wanted, as the apostle Paul writes in Philippians, "to depart and be with Christ, which is better by far." Unlike Paul, I didn't have to remain in the world. No one needed me. They were, whether they knew it or not, better off without me.

A car accident. A brain tumor. A terrorist bomb. Those were my fantasies. People would cry a bit and talk about how I had so much potential. Their memories of me would be fond and simple and unblemished. They would never have to know who I really was, how unlovable, how repulsive.

As time passed and my untimely death never came, I grew more afraid that I would be found out. I prayed harder than ever to change, to become straight, so that if I ever was forced to tell my story, it would be in retrospect. My gay orientation would be the story of who I used to be, before God fixed me. Not the story of who I was.

Change never came.

It wasn't just that God seemed silent when I prayed. It was worse than that. He spoke, and he said no. So I asked again, again, again. Petition after petition and refusal after refusal wore my prayer life thin.

Around the same time, the father of a close friend challenged me to memorize a whole chapter of the Bible. I was a nerd, and a competitive nerd at that, so I did. In a matter of weeks I had memorized Philippians chapter 4, and in a few weeks more I had tacked chapter 3 onto the front. As I rehearsed Paul's words, I began to wonder what they might mean for me:

> I consider everything a loss because of the surpassing worth of knowing Christ Jesus my Lord, for whose sake I have lost all things. . . . Rejoice in the Lord always. . . . The peace of God, which transcends all understanding, will guard your hearts and your minds in Christ Jesus. . . . I have learned the secret of being content in any and every situation, whether well fed or hungry, whether living in plenty or in want. (3:8; 4:4, 7, 12)

I had heard the verses before, but never had I needed them so desperately. In a time when I had almost given up on answers, they felt like the faint beginning of an answer. Perhaps, I thought, this was a request God would grant even when he denied me everything else.

So I stopped praying to be straight. I stopped thinking about my orientation at all, which turned out to be surprisingly easy when all my friends were still unmarried and most of them believed sex before marriage was wrong. Except for my perpetual singleness and my evasive answers in Bible studies whenever the conversation turned to lust, I was no different from anyone else. I was nearly normal. It felt good to be normal.

Instead of praying to like women and to stop liking men, I prayed for joy. I prayed for contentment. I plunged myself so deeply into ministry opportunities, into biblical study, into the lives of others, that I almost managed to forget myself entirely. I became one of the happiest people I knew—happy not just on the surface but all the way through, in love with the world because I was desperately in love with the God who had created it.

I wrote stories and won awards and even got published once or twice. I led worship at my tiny Christian international school, my youth group, my church. I passed my high school classes with flying colors and gave a moving valedictory speech. I had a deep faith, strong friendships, a college scholarship, and a plane ticket to the United States. The future looked bright. It was a wealth, an embarrassment of riches.

To the untrained eye, it looked almost perfect.

But I knew better.

There were still nights of anguish, nights I thought the fault lines between who I was and who I longed to be were sure to erupt and shatter me. I felt dirty, worthless, irredeemable. I would cry, and I would pray, and nothing would change. But in those moments there was always a thread of grace woven into the darkness, and it was always just enough to get me through the night.

2

ALMOST STRAIGHT

THE FIRST TIME WE KISSED, it was raining.

Not storybook rain. Real rain. Wet rain. A cold October drizzle, to be precise—the kind that brought out the earthworms and the smell of New York dirt. It thrummed against the asphalt of the parking lot, rhythmic enough to pass as music, loud enough to give the illusion of privacy.

She held the umbrella. I stood half underneath it, half exposed to the elements, wearing a sodden gray coat I called a raincoat but which was really just the outer shell of a rejected winter coat. The nearest roof couldn't have been more than ten feet away, but we stood in the rain anyway. It seemed like the romantic thing to do.

The kiss had been her idea. Not that I objected. I should have thought of it first, probably, but I didn't. So it was up to her to say bluntly, "Why don't you kiss me?" as she jangled a set of imaginary keys in front of my face.

"Why don't I?" I answered. And I pulled off my sodden gray hood and ducked my head all the way under the umbrella, tilting my chin awkwardly to keep our noses from colliding.

My lips met something warm and soft and strangely human. I held my breath and tried to be in love.

"How was that?" she said.

"Wet," I said, so unromantic I could pass for romantic if I smiled just right.

"For me too. Maybe we need to try again?"

"Let's."

Lips. Warm. Wet. For all the sexual tension I felt, I might as well have been kissing a grapefruit.

I tried adding the tongue. Still nothing.

"Sorry if my technique is poor," I said when I finally pulled away.

"I don't think it's supposed to be about technique," she said.

"No," I agreed. "Of course not."

"But it was nice," she said, giving me the look I should have been giving her.

"Yes," I lied. "It was nice."

■ 🟦 ■

Growing up, I thought of myself as a bad actor. But in college I realized the truth. I was a brilliant actor who had mastered only one role. I was my own alter ego, a bit funnier than the original, a bit friendlier, a bit more resilient. And of course, much less gay.

I played the role well, so well that sometimes I couldn't tell where sincerity ended and acting began. I started to wonder, was there really a difference between the two? Or did I simply become whoever I acted like for long enough? Did I take on the substance of the person I chose to be?

Whenever people asked me why I was still single, I would deliver a carefully worded and well-practiced response: "I feel called to singleness right now. But God is welcome to change my calling anytime."

It was an open-ended answer, and people loved that. "Of *course* you'll get married," they would reassure me. "You just haven't met the right girl yet. Someday you'll meet a girl and she'll make you forget all about your 'calling to singleness.'" They would make the scare quotes with the tones of their voices, as if they doubted there really was such a calling.

Maybe they were right, I thought. Maybe I was just waiting for the right girl. Maybe the right girl would awaken my desires, set me on a course to heterosexual marriage, fix me in a way that all my teenage prayers could not. If that was the case, I was determined to find this girl.

Equally, though, I was terrified. Terrified that there was no such thing as a right girl for me. Terrified that even if I found her, dating her would make me no less gay, and I would break her heart in the end. Or she would break mine. Or I would break my own.

Before college, the closest I had ever come to dating was having what I called "crushes" on girls. They weren't the kinds of crushes my friends were having. There was nothing physical about them, nothing that even came close to approximating heterosexual desire. They were, instead, an especially advanced stage of friendship, an almost clinical assessment of compatibility. If I had to pick a lifelong female partner, I figured, it might as well be someone whose faith and personality and interests aligned neatly with my own. Romance, to the extent that it existed in my brain, was an intellectual phenomenon.

I doubt it ever would have occurred to me to develop these kinds of crushes if I had been left to my own devices. But when it comes to romance, teenagers are never left to their own devices— especially not in the evangelical church. "Who do you *like*?" people would ask me, and I would need a name to give them, a character synopsis, an imagined romance for them to cheer me on in.

"Is she pretty?" they would ask.

"Sure," I would say.

"What does she look like?" they would ask, and I wouldn't have the foggiest idea.

■ 🥚 ■

I attended Roberts Wesleyan College, a small Christian liberal arts college in western New York. Homey and nurturing and academically rigorous all at once, it was the perfect environment for a timid kid fresh off the airplane from Indonesia to learn how to belong. Like any Christian college, Roberts had its share of romantics, those people whose mission was to leave with diploma in hand and spouse on arm. My classmates joked about getting a "ring by spring" or an "MRS degree," but they weren't always joking. The ratio of women to men was about two to one, which meant (as my friends were only too eager to remind me) that the odds were in my favor.

My first college crush was a city girl, smart and personable and energetic. We had long heart-to-hearts late at night, discussing life and theology, exchanging stories and secrets. Before long I was offering her name up to family and friends from home when they called to check in on my love life. She was my shibboleth, continuing proof that I could be normal.

Our relationship-defining talk came on a late fall evening in my freshman year, during a walk around the perimeter of campus. We were just passing the soccer field when I started trying to ease into the topic, as my tongue turned dry and grainy.

"I know we both said we enjoyed being single in college, and we wanted to stay that way for a while . . ."

"Absolutely," she agreed, rendering my whole script beyond that point worthless. I regrouped.

"But I've been thinking," I said. "If I ever were going to date someone here, I think I would want it to be you."

"I guess I feel the same," she said. "Not that I want to date anyone. But if I did, you're definitely my closest guy friend here."

We went on talking about friendship, about life. I walked her back to her dorm room and said goodnight. That was the end of it.

Lacking experience with romantic conversations, I simply assumed that this one qualified. She desired me in exactly the same way I desired her: as a good friend, the sort of person I wouldn't mind sharing apartments with for the rest of my life. Wasn't that love?

It took me by surprise when, several weeks later, she announced to me her interest in a mutual friend of ours. "Do you think he likes me?" she asked. "Should I be more obvious? Am I being too obvious?"

Meanwhile, our mutual friend was asking me the same questions. "She sent me this text message . . . what do you think? Should I make a move?"

My crush was suddenly a different person from the one I had circled campus with. Her ambitions of singleness in college had all disappeared. And so had my status as the guy she was most likely to date. This new guy had what I didn't, an allure, a spark I didn't understand.

So I did what I assumed any caring friend would do in the same situation. I helped set them up with each other. I hinted to each of them that their feelings might be reciprocated. I organized hangouts for the three of us and then made myself scarce once we were all together. I watched their relationship blossom.

And it barely even hurt.

That was love, I thought, wasn't it? To care enough that you just wanted her to be happy, even if it wasn't with you? That didn't make me gay.

I watched them start dating, watched them fall in love, watched them get married. It was beautiful. It was easy. Too easy.

■ ◙ ■

If my "crushes" were girls I could imagine marrying, then I had no word to describe the people who made my head turn and left me feeling weak in the knees. They were all guys. There could be no future with them. As long as I didn't have a word—as long as my brain lacked a category—I could pretend they didn't exist.

But they did exist. I admired them from a distance, greeted them as we crossed paths between classes, chatted with them over meals. I rarely became very close with them. They seemed mystical and unreachable. Maybe even dangerous.

In the college vocabulary most familiar to me, same-sex attraction existed only as a punch line. Homoerotic banter and behavior were seen as normal ways of reaffirming masculinity. Some residents of Miner Hall, the all-male dorm where I lived during my freshman year, roamed the halls in various states of undress, embracing each other, riding scooters naked, wolf-whistling and catcalling. When guys offered me compliments, they were usually joking come-ons: "You're a beautiful man. What's cookin', good-lookin'? You sexy beast."

I absorbed the culture, chameleonlike, and learned to return the compliments with equal levity. "Hey there, hot stuff," I would say, trying not to notice their sometimes beautiful bodies, trying not to mean what I said any more than they did. I almost always succeeded.

Almost.

Almost is a cheap word, a Benedict Arnold, ready to abandon you at a moment's notice. There's no assurance if you're only almost sure. There's no rest.

As soon as I got the chance, I moved out of the dorms and into an apartment, where the nudity was less ubiquitous and no one pretended to make sexual advances on me in the hallways.

I took an introductory psychology class one semester with several good friends. We were studying for an exam in the library, going over the chapter on sexuality, when we ran across an infographic that showed the professions with the highest concentrations of LGBTQ-identifying individuals. Second on the list, at 26 percent, was fiction writing.

"Hey," said one of my friends, looking up at me. "You write fiction, don't you?"

I winked. "Oh yes," I said, "I am a fiction writer."

We all laughed, and it became a running joke. In our group parlance, "fiction writer" became synonymous with "gay." The fact that I really had written fiction—that I could be the butt of this meaningless joke about sexuality—that was the best part of all.

It was hilarious. At least, my alter ego thought it was hilarious. And when he laughed, I laughed.

■ 🔲 ■

Looking back, it seems strange to me that the thought of coming out, of admitting my fraught experience of sexuality, barely even occurred to me in college. The role I acted never seemed like a conscious decision. It was a default, a factory setting. Pretending to be straight was the only way I knew how to be what I was and still follow Jesus as I understood him.

It didn't help that I'd never heard of anyone else whose experience of sexuality was quite like mine, let alone met them or known them personally. I knew about two kinds of gay Christians: the ones who revised the traditional interpretation of the Bible's stance on homosexual behavior in order to pursue committed same-sex relationships, and the ones who repented after years of promiscuity and became straight—the "ex-gays." Neither category included me. I was, as far as I knew, alone.

Meanwhile, there were all sorts of fears to keep me quiet. What would my friends think, especially my male friends? Would they hold me at arm's length out of disdain, or perhaps with the best of intentions, to spare me the risk of falling in love with them? If I lost every opportunity for healthy same-sex intimacy, wouldn't that just make the problem worse?

And what about my leadership roles? I was leading worship and speaking about my faith in increasingly public contexts. Would I lose the ability to reach those people? Would I create a rift in my community, turn from a success story into a tragedy?

Besides, I wasn't going to stay gay, not forever. I was going to find the legendary right girl, desire her, marry her, choose to be straight. As long as I kept my mouth shut, my sexuality might be as protean as my career goals and my tastes in music.

Admitting made everything too real, too permanent.

So I held my tongue and acted my way through college. It wasn't that I lied, mind you—I wouldn't have stood for that—but I spoke the truth strategically. I told the part of the story I was ready to tell and replaced the rest of it with tangents and big words and wide smiles. I learned to do what I had always longed to do: blend in.

Where I had grown up in Indonesia, blending in was impossible. I was the lone white face in a sea of chocolate, a too-tall, blond-haired, blue-eyed sore thumb. Over the phone I could pass for a native, my perfect Indonesian accent disguising my misfit body. But in person, everyone knew I didn't quite belong. I may have acted like one of them, but my skin proved that I would always be an American.

During high school I got myself to school and back using a public transportation system called *angkot*, a buslike network of minivans with the back seats removed and two long benches set in their place. As I walked a kilometer to the nearest *angkot* stop each morning, neighborhood kids would shout their limited English at me: "Halo Mister! What is your name? You crazy! I love you!" I would smile through gritted teeth and nod at the kids, whose parents nodded apologetically back at me.

My experience wasn't what we in America would call racial discrimination. Quite the opposite, in fact—I was a privileged minority, richer and better educated than all my neighbors, envied by them. But no matter how privileged, the minority is still a lonely place to be.

College was the first place I discovered the magic of fitting in. No one called me "albino" in the streets or gaped at me as I walked by. But even in my biological homeland, surrounded by sweet anonymity, I knew I didn't quite belong. People would find out where I had grown up, or catch me speaking a hybrid US/Canadian/Australian/British English, or realize my ineptitude with American popular culture, and my cover would be blown. I would be unceremoniously thrust back behind the bars of the orangutan cage, an object of wonder and curiosity and amazement to be intensely scrutinized.

Since the age of three, one of my deepest desires had been to fit in somewhere, to find a place I could belong, to be "normal." But how, I wondered, could I be normal as a white-skinned Indonesian whose sense of home was only as permanent as the location of my toothbrush?

How could I be normal if I admitted to being gay?

I knew what it felt like to stick out, to be different, to have people stare at me in shock as I passed by. It would have taken a kind of courage to willingly thrust myself into yet another minority. And it was a courage I was sure I didn't have.

I found my normalcy in bits and pieces, one day at a time, one friendship, one community. In the places I found it, I clung to it jealously, crouching Gollum-like over it and calling it precious. I would have done almost anything to hang on to it.

So I kept acting, and acting, until eventually I acted my way into a dating relationship, the magic bullet that was supposed to turn my life around.

■ ● ■

Imagine (if you're straight) being told that you had to marry one of your closest same-sex friends. Imagine trying to pick one, trying to convince yourself that you were more attracted to that one than to all the rest. Imagine wondering if it would one day become your spousal duty to have sex with that person, no matter how nauseating and strange the thought seemed. Imagine approaching them, telling them you had some special affection for them, and waiting breathlessly for a response, not sure if you wanted the green light or the glowing red.

That strange mixture of revulsion and desire and terror and indifference: that was what I felt when I started dating. As I declared my love (didn't we all love each other in Christ anyway?), I wanted everything to be different. I was counting on everything becoming different. But nothing was. Not yet.

So I kept acting.

The place it was hardest to act, as it turned out, was in a dating relationship. Holding hands, cuddling, kissing—I had to be reminded that they were a normal part of most relationships, something my girlfriend might want and expect, something I was supposed to want. I did them dutifully but mechanically, teaching myself the motions as I went along, like a child learning an instrument or painting by numbers.

As I went through the motions of romance, I tried to teach myself to want them. I prayed to want them.

And really, I should have wanted them. I knew, on an intellectual level, that my girlfriend was beautiful. She was also one of my closest college friends, brilliant but not arrogant, caring but not clingy. For three years, we pulled an all-nighter every spring to write a one-act play together. She was so easy to be with. I loved the person I became when I was with her.

I should have been in love. But I wasn't.

One night the two of us were sitting and talking in the living room of my apartment when my roommate came downstairs. "I see you're enjoying my couch," he said.

"Good couch," we agreed.

"I'm going out," he said. "Whatever you do, don't you dare make out on my couch."

Ah, the power of suggestion.

As soon as the door closed, my girlfriend turned to me. "Want to make out on his couch?"

I didn't want to, not really. But I wanted to want to.

"Obviously," I said, and then we were entangled. I tried to lose myself in the moment. I willed myself to become aroused. I breathed through my nose, feeling the intimacy of my own discarded breath as it bounced off her cheek and wafted back to me.

She pulled back, guided my hand from her shoulder to her waist. "That's better," she said.

I would have agreed, but our lips were interlocked again. I wondered how long was normal to make out for. Two minutes? Five? How would I know when to stop? I started counting seconds.

Her hands ran the length of my back. It tickled. It was pleasurable. I couldn't be sure, but it might have been a spark of heterosexual desire. I tried to hang onto the feeling, tried to augment it in my mind.

When we finally pulled away and whispered our breathless goodnights, I felt a damp spot on my boxers, pressed against my thigh. It was proof that I had felt something. Proof I was turning straight. And that was good, wasn't it? It was worth celebrating?

If it was good, why did I feel so filthy? Why was half my heart sinking while the other half leaped for joy?

I fell asleep praying hybrid prayers that were at once thanksgiving and repentance. "Thanks for starting to make me straight," I said to God. "Please keep going. Please don't stop." And in the same breath: "I'm sorry. Is this lust? I can't tell anymore. I don't know what I want. But I know I want what you want."

When I got out of bed the next morning, the damp spot on my boxers had dried up, and with it had disappeared the only shred of heterosexual desire I ever felt.

■ ◆ ■

There are few parts of my life I'm more ashamed of than this one. Ashamed for being willing to do almost anything to awaken the sexual desires I thought I deserved. Ashamed for the way I used her, made her the subject of my failed science experiment. Ashamed that in the days and weeks that followed, as she doubted her own beauty because of my inability to want her, I still held my tongue.

We broke up not long afterward. There were other reasons for the breakup, reasons that seemed urgently important at the time, reasons that I forced myself to believe were the only reasons. But underneath everything else was a subtext I couldn't speak aloud. Most of the time, I didn't even dare to think it.

I had tried to be straight, and I had failed. I was so close. I was almost straight. But *almost* is a cheap word.

One of the first times we saw each other after the breakup, I was making applesauce in my tiny apartment kitchen. A cheap aluminum pot I had bought for twenty-five cents at a garage sale bubbled happily on the stove, full of apples smuggled out of the dining hall in my backpack. It smelled like autumn. But the smell was deceptive, because temperatures had already begun to drop below freezing and everyone knew autumn was dying.

We talked about the decay that had so recently seemed like a thriving relationship. It was painful and tense, and every word was heavy with too much meaning.

Was there a chance we would ever get back together? Probably not. Could we still be friends? Maybe. Would it ever be the same as it had been before? If only.

I offered her a mug of apple water, the pale pink nectar poured off a too-juicy batch of apples.

"You know," she said, keeping her voice light so that it sounded like she was joking, "all this would be so much easier if you were gay."

Part of me wanted to admit it. But when you're not ready to come out to the world—when you haven't even really admitted it to yourself yet—the most dangerous person you can possibly come out to is your ex-girlfriend.

"I'm sorry," I said, hoping she understood my words as a denial and not a confession.

She took a sip from the steaming mug. "I'm going to vomit," she said.

"Are you talking about us, or about the apple water?" I asked.

She put the mug down on the counter, moved toward the door. "You decide."

■ ▧ ■

A year passed before I came close to dating again. I was fresh out of college and working for a small church in upstate New York, in a town so far north that it felt to me more like Canada than New York. This time my crush was a gifted worship leader with a magnetic personality. She shared my obsession for music theory, and together we sang the best duets I've ever sung. We talked and laughed easily with each other. She emanated passion like it was something palpable, like currents tugging under the surface of a river. She inspired me, made me want to be the finest version of myself.

I had once heard someone define Christian marriage as a union between a man and woman who serve God better together than they could have as individuals. If there was ever a woman with whom I could inhabit this definition, I thought, she would be the one.

The night we discovered our mutual interest in each other, we had just finished playing and singing for an outreach event at a local college campus. We set off on a four-hour walk through the campus and the surrounding town, both of us knowing we needed to talk, neither one knowing quite what to say.

I hadn't meant to bare my soul to her. But I was more afraid of making the same mistake twice—of destroying another friendship in my quest to become straight—than I was of telling the truth.

So I told her everything, drew her into a confidence she hadn't asked for. "Everybody has to fight attractions once they get married," I said. "And I could fight my attractions for guys just like any other guy would fight his attraction for girls. But that wouldn't be fair to you, would it? You're beautiful. I know that. But I might not ever desire you that way. And there are so many great guys who would desire you, who already do desire you. So we shouldn't be together, should we?"

"I don't know," she said. "Do you think you could ever change?"

"I don't know," I said. "I would try to change. For you, I would try to make it work."

"Me too," she said.

We agreed to pray about it. I walked her home. And for two weeks I thought and hoped and dreamed of becoming straight and marrying someone like her.

No, not someone *like* her. I dreamed of marrying her, herself, and no one else.

But when I closed my eyes to pray my dreams into reality, I saw Jesus shaking his head in the darkness.

"You don't understand," I begged him. "This is my chance. There's no woman I could possibly want to marry more than her. If you don't say yes now, you probably never will, and I'll be gay and alone for the rest of my life."

"I know," he said, and there were tears on his cheeks to match the tears on mine.

I gave her a call and met her for coffee later that week.

"If your answer is yes, my answer is yes," she said.

I was on the verge of saying what we both wanted to hear. But I couldn't quite form the words. "I'm sorry," I said. "I think God is telling me no."

"Oh," she said.

"Maybe it will change," I said. "I want it to change. But it's not fair to ask you to wait for that."

"No," she said, "I guess not."

"I'm sorry I'm not who I wish I was," I said.

"Don't be sorry," she said. "It's not your fault."

A few months later, with my knowledge and support, a mutual friend of ours asked her out. She said yes. Then the dating, the engagement, the marriage, the happily ever after. It was beautiful and perfect, everything I could have wished for them both. They were, and remain, some of my dearest friends.

But that didn't mean my heart couldn't break just a bit. So I let it break.

It was like watching someone else have the life I could have had, as my own fragile dreams smoldered and crumbled and drifted away like ash.

■3■

DEBATING THE DIVINE

AFTER THAT FINAL NO, as I laid my dreams of marriage and family to rest, perhaps forever, I was the angriest I've ever been with God. No less in love. No less willing to follow. But furious and desperate and confused.

I had a right to be straight, didn't I? Wasn't that implied by the Bible's mandates against homosexuality? Most of the Christians I knew seemed to think so: that there was no such thing as being born gay; that God was just waiting to spring heterosexuality onto anyone who asked; that if you stayed gay, it was probably your own fault. Not that they said as much. But it was written into their voices as they declared God's stance on the issue, as they painted "the homosexuals" with a wide-bristle brush of condemnation.

Could they have been wrong?

And if they were wrong about that, what else might they have been wrong about?

Since those fateful puberty days when I first began to come to terms with my sexuality, there were two assumptions I had never spent much time questioning. The first was that Jesus was real, loved me, died for me, left words in the Bible for me to live by. The second was that the Bible declared homosexual behavior a sin.

For a few dark days, I haggled with the first assumption. But in the end I couldn't let it go. Too much of my experience had proved my faith to be true. Too much of my life made sense only through the lens of the gospel story. To throw away everything I believed and understood—to plunge the rest of my world into darkness in order to make sense of one shadow—I could think of no fate worse than that.

Then came the second assumption.

I had inspected the Bible's assessment of homosexuality before—how could I not have, being what I was?—but until now it had only been a cursory inspection, to confirm what I already thought was true. I had never deconstructed my own assumptions, started from scratch, read with fresh eyes.

Did I dare to open that door? For most of the evangelical community I was steeped in, acknowledging the sinfulness of homosexuality was a litmus test of biblical belief, and therefore a test of true faith. Affirming gay marriage was synonymous with discarding the Bible. It felt like a sin even to ask the question.

But I couldn't help asking it. I needed to know, and not just to take for granted what someone else had told me. I needed to see it for myself.

So I ordered books and watched YouTube videos and dusted off my Greek New Testament, and I dared to think the unthinkable.

■ ● ■

Those of us who come from an evangelical background and adhere to traditional interpretations of the Bible usually don't like to admit that we're interpreting at all. We're simply reading and understanding. It's all the other people—the people we disagree with—

who are interpreting. "God said it," runs our bumper-sticker-friendly mantra. "I believe it. That settles it." Our hermeneutic lens, the framework through which we approach and analyze Scripture, is so straightforward it becomes almost flippant.

I'm not faulting the heart behind this hermeneutic lens—I think the people who invoke it are usually sincere and want more than anything to follow Jesus. I don't even disagree with many of the stances they adopt via this attitude. The pervasiveness of sin. The divinity and supremacy of Christ. The urgency of evangelism. I affirm these truths. I celebrate whenever and however people come to believe them. But even so, the bumper-sticker hermeneutic worries me for two reasons.

First, reading the Bible this way reveals the shallowness of our love for God's Word. Sometimes we're so in love with easy answers and calendar-sized sound bites that we fall out of love with the Bible itself. We overlook the messy, the nuanced, the complicated. Or we try to read the Bible like a systematic theology, smoothing over the lumps with a rolling pin, forgetting that God could have given us a systematic theology if he wanted to, and he instead chose to give us something unsystematic, something dangerous.

Second, the bumper-sticker hermeneutic leaves us helpless where the Bible seems to contradict itself. How do we respond when the order of creation changes between Genesis 1 and Genesis 2? When kidnapping and enslaving people is condemned, but slaves are told to obey their masters? When Paul appears to forbid women from filling leadership roles in the church and then speaks highly of women who have taken on leadership roles? The logic of surface meaning forces us to read dismissively, to overlook or explain away whatever doesn't seem to fit. We miss the opportunity to read holistically because we're too busy regrouping, cutting our losses, trying to protect the Bible from itself.

I say this not to defend revisionary readings of the Bible's approach to homosexuality but to defend the instinct that makes us bold enough to raise the question. If we truly love Scripture, we have to love it enough to let it prove us wrong.

And at the same time, we have to love it enough to let it tell us what we don't want to hear.

■ ● ■

For too long, the message I heard and believed about homosexuality in the Bible was simply this: "Paul says practicing homosexuals won't inherit the kingdom of God. So gay sex is a sin. End of story. #insertdefinitivehashtaghere."

If that had been the whole story, I could have accepted it and moved on. But as I learned once I started to read, it wasn't the whole story. The case against homosexual behavior wasn't as clearcut as I'd been trained to believe. Because language and translation are complicated things.

I began my research with Paul's famous lists prohibiting same-sex behavior in 1 Corinthians 6 and 1 Timothy 1. Since Paul had neither the luxury of English nor a twenty-first-century conception of sexual behavior, I realized, it was functionally impossible to offer a twenty-first-century English rendering of these passages that would mean precisely the same thing. The Greek word often rendered "homosexual offenders" or "practicing homosexuals" in English is *arsenokoitai*, a compound formed from the Greek words *arsēn*, male, and *koitē*, bed. A man-bedder. Obviously a homosexual, right?

Probably. But no responsible language scholar would call it a slam dunk. The problem with assuming we understand this word is that Paul's two uses are the first times the word appears anywhere in the Greek corpus we now have access to. And we can't go assuming that the parts of a compound word point irrevocably to the whole, unless we're ready to assert that the English poets who praised the butterfly were thrilled by winged dairy products.

What about Leviticus 18 and 20, I wondered, where God declares that for men to lie together is an "abomination" (*toebah* in Hebrew)? Wasn't an abomination something so bad that it would always be forbidden, even under the new covenant of Christ? Again, a careful linguistic analysis made my life more complicated. Deuteronomy 14 used the same word, *toebah*, to describe unclean foods forbidden to the Hebrew people—foods Jesus would later declare clean to true God-followers.

I read with burgeoning hopefulness, burgeoning enthusiasm. The story of Sodom in Genesis 19—perhaps it wasn't about same-sex attraction but about gang rape. Indeed, the prophet Ezekiel's later assessment of Sodom had nothing to do with homosexuality: "Now this was the sin of your sister Sodom: She and her daughters were arrogant, overfed and unconcerned; they did not help the poor and needy" (16:49). And Romans 1—it seemed Paul's primary interest was in rebellion against God, not homosexuality. Perhaps he was simply referencing familiar practices of temple prostitution or the famous perversions of the Roman emperor Caligula for illustrative purposes.

That was it: six biblical references to homosexuality. That was all I needed to explain away in order to hang on to my faith and still have everything I wanted.

I could almost believe it. I prayed that if it was really true, God would set me free to believe it. That he would give me peace and assurance at the thought of a covenantal same-sex relationship. That my lingering doubts would all be replaced by joy and confidence.

I prayed, and God seemed to shake his head. There was no peace. The doubts grew instead of shrinking.

The Bible's treatment of homosexuality was complicated, yes. More complicated than the well-meaning conservative preachers and ex-gay ministers were ready to admit. But the fact that it was complicated didn't make every interpretation equally valid. There was still a best way of reading the text, still a truth that deserved to be pursued.

And when I pursued it, I got the answer I feared, not the answer I wanted. More and more, I found myself believing that the Bible's call to me was a call to self-denial through celibacy.

I was still sympathetic to the revisionist argument that affirmed the possibility of same-sex marriage. Part of me still wanted to believe it, and I understood at the most visceral level why some sincere Christians might choose to adopt this view. But no matter how much I sympathized, how well I tried to understand, there were a few essential ideas that rang hollow to me.

■ ● ■

First, there was the issue of suffering.

Some of the most eloquent and passionate Christian advocates of same-sex marriage I had encountered were those who spoke of gay celibacy as a cataclysmic burden. "How can we force this suffering on people?" they asked. "Aren't we like the Pharisees, placing unbearable loads on people's shoulders, when we require gay people to stay celibate? Doesn't the incredible pain caused by the homosexual prohibition prove there's something amiss with the traditional reading of Scripture?"

On the one hand, much of what they said was true. It was true that the road of the celibate gay Christian had been, as I knew it so far, an excruciating one. It was true that being asked to ignore something so central to my identity seemed at times like an impossible request. It was true that I had despaired, considered giving up on God, wanted to die.

But none of that meant that the traditional interpretation of the Bible was wrong.

Obedience is supposed to be costly. When Jesus told his followers to take up their crosses and follow him, he wasn't just calling them to place heftier checks in the offering plate or to put up with the occasional irritation at work. He was calling them to blood and sorrow and unspeakable agony. He was calling them to death.

In many parts of the world, this calling to death is still very much a literal one for those who declare their allegiance to Christ. And if not death, perhaps the risk of beatings, of deprivation, of complete ostracization by family and community. But in the Western world, lulled by freedom of religion and unprecedented opulence, we so easily lose sight of what words like *suffering* really mean. We begin to believe that ease and safety are the baseline experiences of humanity, the natural states of being from which any other state diverges. And suffering, when it comes, feels like a violation. Suffering shocks us.

"I'll follow you," we say to Christ so readily, watching the thorns dig into his forehead. And then, moments later, we cry foul when we discover thorns of our own.

Don't let the aesthetically pleasing cross hanging around your neck or on the wall of your church building fool you. There was nothing sanitary about the cross. Nothing beautiful, except the beautiful scandal of our redemption.

Maybe the problem isn't that gay Christians have received an impossible task. Maybe the problem is that so many straight Christians have given themselves a task that is too easy, a cross that's too bearable. While gay Christians are expected to deny themselves in their desires for sex and family and intimacy—desires that feel so intrinsically part of their being—most straight Christians can simply channel those desires toward a single woman or man, get married, have kids, join a country club, attend a welcoming church where everything has been designed with people like them in mind, and chase the Jesus-festooned brand of the American dream.

I don't mean to belittle the self-denial necessary to a God-honoring, monogamous heterosexual marriage. Remaining faithful to a single partner is no small feat (or so I'm told). And certainly some straight Christians who desire marriage may yet find themselves called to celibacy. Regardless of orientation, regardless of marital status, Christ's invitation to the cross remains no less true, no less necessary.

But the road of celibacy for the gay Christian remains a distinctly complex calling. To not only resist sexual urges but to try to banish the thought of ever fulfilling them. To have no daydreams of a future romance, no wistful marriage plans. To feel like the very core of your sexual desire and the faith you hold most dear are at odds with each other. There are sufferings far worse than this, but there is none quite the same. My heart has its own fracture lines, its own unique ways of breaking.

And maybe that's not a bad thing.

Maybe the calling to gay Christian celibacy stands in twenty-first-century America as a precious reminder of just how desperately, helplessly devoted we were meant to be to the cross of Christ. A reminder that every sacrifice we make will pale in comparison to the sacrifice made on our behalf.

Maybe the problem isn't that faith costs some of us too much, but that it costs all of us too little.

■ ◉ ■

Then, in addition to suffering, there was the issue of silence.

Gay-marriage-affirming interpretations of the Bible, at their most persuasive, sought to prove the Bible's silence on the topic of committed same-sex relationships. The biblical writers had no concept of sexual orientation, they argued. Jesus never once mentioned the issue. Once the Bible's silence on the particulars had been established, we could use general principles (the "it is not good for the man to be alone" of Genesis 2:18, or Galatians 5:14's "the entire law is fulfilled in keeping this one command: 'Love your neighbor as yourself'") to establish a positive case for same-sex marriage. Once six misunderstood passages had been explained, then the whole Bible would be silent about me.

And that, I realized, was the most intolerable thought of all.

To be forgotten. To be accidentally excluded. To be of such little value that even Jesus, who championed minorities fiercely and offended the privileged majority by the radical reach of his love and attention, decided I wasn't worth mentioning.

For me, the idea of being forgotten was worse than the call to celibacy.

So I started asking a different question of the Bible. If Jesus knew about people like me, I asked—if he meant to speak even to someone whose experience of sexuality resembled mine—then how might he have said it in front of a crowd of Jews two thousand years ago?

Though Jesus himself never answers the question of whether the old covenant's prohibition of homosexual behavior is meant to extend into the new covenant, he does make a general reaffirmation of the old covenant's sexual ethics when he speaks in Matthew 15 (and the parallel passage in Mark 7) of sexual immorality, *porneia*, alongside crimes like murder and adultery, as a product of the brokenness of the human heart. An audience of Jews, specifically Jesus' own disciples, would likely have understood this term as shorthand for all the forms of sexual behavior forbidden by the Levitical law. The apostles in Jerusalem make a similar affirmation of Levitical sexual ethics in Acts 15, when they decide that *porneia* is one of four essential old covenant prohibitions they will encourage Gentile believers to avoid.

Not only does Jesus speak against sexual immorality as Jews would have understood it, but he also reaffirms the sanctity of the marriage bond between male and female. In Matthew 19 (paralleled in Mark 10), when Pharisees come to question him about Moses' divorce laws, Jesus explains that the marital mystery in which "the two become one flesh" is rooted in the creation story. "Haven't you read," he says, "that at the beginning the Creator 'made them male and female?'" (Matthew 19:4). Given the opportunity to define the basis and purpose of Christian marriage, Jesus points to the sexual beauty of men and women, as distinct expressions of the divine image, being united to reflect the fullness of God.

As I continued to study and pray and wrestle with God, I found more and more that seemed to confirm this view. Paul might have had a specific cultural moment in mind in Romans 1, but his language is much broader than that, stretching to include all homosexual behavior. The compound word *arsenokoitai*, the word sometimes translated "homosexuals," which appears in 1 Corinthians 6 and 1 Timothy 1, mimics the phrasing of the Septuagint, a Greek translation of the Old Testament that was being circulated in Paul's day. The Septuagint's rendering of the prohibitions in Leviticus 18 and 20 uses the terms *arsēn* and *koitē*, the same terms from which Paul coins his new word, even though there are more common Greek words for both maleness and sexual activity. Assuming Paul's word choice is strategic, it's nearly certain that Paul meant to reaffirm the sinfulness of same-sex behavior outlined in Leviticus.

So then, Jesus knew me after all. He hadn't forgotten me. He had known what I would want, how urgently I would want it, how it would seem at times to overtake every thought. And he had responded that the desires I had weren't meant to be fulfilled. Not in this life. He had called me to self-denial, to sorrow.

He had called me to a cross.

It was an answer. Not the answer I wanted, but an answer all the same. And perhaps any answer at all was better than none.

■ ● ■

For a little while I was satisfied. But then, before the ink on my interim vows of celibacy had dried, I was back to my old refrain, demanding that God turn me straight. How could he make the deepest desires of my heart be the very things I couldn't have? How could he leave me broken? If he hadn't forgotten me, then why was he refusing to heal me? Where was that in the Bible?

I asked the last question petulantly, wanting a rationale for self-pity more than I wanted an answer. But God, who likes to take people literally, gave me an answer anyway, buried in a passage from 2 Corinthians 12 that I'd read and quoted a hundred times before:

> Therefore, in order to keep me from becoming conceited, I was given a thorn in my flesh, a messenger of Satan, to torment me. Three times I pleaded with the Lord to take it away from me. But he said to me, "My grace is sufficient for you, for my power is made perfect in weakness." Therefore I will boast all the more gladly about my weaknesses, so that Christ's power may rest on me. That is why, for Christ's sake, I delight in weaknesses, in insults, in hardships, in persecutions, in difficulties. For when I am weak, then I am strong. (vv. 7-10)

God, it seemed, had never quite agreed with Paul on what counted as "weakness." While Paul was begging for healing, God was celebrating an opportunity to show off his strength. While Paul was busy wishing away the parts of his story that felt like unrepaired brokenness, God was redefining brokenness and wholeness at the foot of the cross.

When Paul finally found delight, he found it not in spite of his thorns, but because of them.

And if that was true, I realized, perhaps it wasn't wrong for me to struggle either. Perhaps it wasn't wrong to face a challenge I could never seem to defeat. Whether or not God had designed me this way, he was fully within his rights when he allowed me a predisposition to things I could never have, fully within his rights when he refused to "fix" me. God's denials didn't make my prayers deficient. His silences didn't make him absent.

Being gay didn't mean God had rejected me. Maybe it was just a thorn in my flesh, an invitation to frailty, a unique kind of weakness.

And maybe that weakness was also a unique kind of strength, a unique invitation to delight.

There were no fireworks that came with this revelation. I didn't throw a dance party or go shouting my orientation from the rooftops. I still didn't want to be gay. There was still wrestling and sorrow and lament that refused to leave, that would perhaps never cease to be part of my experience of faith.

But I began to realize that my sexual orientation was an inextricable part of the bigger story God was telling over my life. My interests, my passions, my abilities, my temperament, my calling—there was no way to sever those things completely from the gay desires and mannerisms and attitudes that had developed alongside them. For the first time in my life, I felt free to celebrate the beautiful mess I had become.

Slowly, stumblingly, I learned to take delight in the person God had allowed me to be. Weak. Tormented. Dependent. Strong.

Loved.

■4■

WHAT GOD
CALLED GOOD

HERE'S A FUN EXPERIMENT YOU CAN TRY AT HOME: invite your favorite
local theologian out to coffee and ask him or her whether mosquitoes were created before the fall.

My dad and I used to haggle over this question when I was
growing up. Indonesia has no shortage of mosquitoes, and my dad
hates them—hates them with such a passion that it's almost spiritual. Whenever he kills one, he rejoices loudly over the tiny corpse
smeared on his hand. "Bless God!" he'll yell. Or "The Lord gives
me victory over my enemies!" Or, in the bellicose spirit of the
Psalms, "May all my enemies be like that mosquito!"

(There are very few animals you can kill gleefully without being
called a sociopath—but nobody cares when you kill mosquitoes.
There are no mosquito rights activists.)

If mosquitoes are essentially parasitic and vile in nature—if all
they're good for is sucking blood and spreading disease and making
you itch and whining in your ears—then how could they have existed
in the Garden of Eden? How could God have included them when
he was handing out blue ribbons to everything and announcing how
good it all was?

So we would speculate, my father and I. Were mosquitoes a late addition to the creation game, along with earthquakes and Alzheimer's disease and New Jersey traffic? Were they the spawn of Satan, fully distinct from God's original creative vision? Or was there such a thing as a good mosquito? Was there a form of mosquito, before the fall, that manifested a unique facet of God's glory?

Maybe, I liked to imagine, the mosquito's bite used to mean something entirely different before the world went wrong. Maybe the exchange of blood was seen as an act of love, and Adam and Eve and the animals used to look forward to the privilege of sharing the life in their veins with their mosquito friends. Maybe the red welts that mosquitoes left behind were like souvenirs, like party favors, treasured residues of a place where love had been.

It's hard when we see things now, through the opaque lens of sin, to imagine what the original was meant to be.

■ ▪ ■

What would a person like me have looked like before the fall, or if the fall had never happened? Would I have been straight just like everyone else? Does being gay mean that I'm one step further away from God's design, my desires just a bit more disordered than everyone else's?

That's certainly what the evangelical church taught me to believe. Gay orientation—or, for those who didn't use the language of orientation, same-sex attraction—was a special brand of human fallenness, evidence of just how bad the world had become. It was something to be ashamed of, something to pray away, with hopes that it would be replaced by safer, more predictable forms of heterosexual sinfulness. The best possible evidence that Christ had shown up in a gay person's life was for that person to become straight.

This line of reasoning contained enough truth that I almost accepted it. Humankind is deeply, devastatingly fallen—I believed that. My homosexual orientation was broken—I believed that.

But wasn't heterosexual orientation broken too?

I had seen the pornography my straight friends were captivated by. I had heard men talk about women as if they were competitions to be won, as if they were aerosol canisters to be used up and discarded. It made me sick. Those men were broken in ways I had never been, just as I was broken in places where they were whole.

It sometimes felt strange to me, having dear friends who loved me offer to lay hands on me and pray with me that I would exchange one form of brokenness for another.

Is it possible, I finally dared to ask myself, that homosexuality isn't merely a disordered form of heterosexuality? That instead *every* sexual orientation after the fall is a disordered form of original sexuality as God had intended it to be? Our ways of interacting with one another, the places we seek intimacy and the places we ignore it, the beauty we appreciate and the beauty we overlook—everything has gone wrong.

Gay men see women wrong. Gay men see other men wrong. But then again, straight men see women wrong too. Straight men see other men wrong. Women of any orientation see women wrong, see men wrong. We are all guilty of exchanging healthy intimacy for ravenous sexuality or emotional distance. We are all, if left to our own devices, bound to miss the rich potpourri of relationship and love we were created for.

Is it too dangerous, too unorthodox, to believe that I am uniquely designed to reflect the glory of God? That my orientation, before the fall, was meant to be a gift in appreciating the beauty of my own sex as I celebrated the friendship of the opposite sex? That perhaps even within God's flawless original design there might have been eunuchs, people called to lives of holy singleness?

We in the church recoil from the word *gay*, from the very notion of same-sex orientation, because we know what it looks like only outside of Eden, where everything has gone wrong. But what if there's goodness hiding within the ruins? What if the calling to gay Christian celibacy is more than just a failure of straightness? What if God dreamed it for me, wove it into the fabric of my being as he knit me together and sang life into me?

Is it possible for me to continue pursuing wholeness in Christ even if I stop praying to be straight?

■ ▉ ■

I started cutting my own hair during my senior year of college. It was cheap and efficient, two things I cared about more than the quality of the final product. And because I could do it whenever I wanted, it saved me from the indignity of letting my hair grow too long and reach what I called "the baby chick phase," the point at which it refused to lie flat and instead puffed into a ball of dander, soft and blond and unpredictable.

The clippers were borrowed from a friend. They were old, weak. They tugged painfully on my scalp if I wasn't careful. I figured out which attachment was best to use through trial and error, which meant that I spent a few weeks in the spring looking like a skinhead, like an oddly scrawny army recruit.

Every month or two, when I sensed I was approaching the dreaded baby chick phase, I would borrow the clippers again, strip down to my boxers in front of the bathroom mirror, and stare myself down for ten minutes as the clippers tugged and moaned and tiny hairs cascaded onto the tile floor. I would learn myself, the moles, the pimples, the immutable love handles. I would gaze into the eyes of a gay man as those eyes gazed into mine.

"Who do you wish you were?" I would whisper sometimes, and the man in the mirror would whisper the same haunting question back.

I would look at myself and wonder what God had seen in me back in the Garden of Eden, back when he declared that his handiwork was very good. Had he known, when he spoke those words, the thing I would become? Had he known the lusts I would fight, the trysts with a pornography that was somehow worse than other people's pornography, the broken desires that seemed to disqualify me from marriage or romance or intimacy? Had he known that there would be nights I would resent him and curse him and choose to pretend he didn't exist?

Was it possible that he could have known all this and still called me good?

When I looked at myself in the mirror, I saw a mosquito, a creature gone fundamentally wrong. But God had known me in the days when even mosquitoes were beautiful.

❖

I'm not necessarily trying to say that God made me gay, as if it's somehow his fault that I struggle in the ways I do, or as if he owes it to me to let me act on my desires. I'm not even trying to say that mosquitoes were the life of every party in the Garden of Eden. What I want to say, more than anything else, is that I don't know. I don't know what the world looked like before we broke God's heart. I don't know what it was God saw in me, when he pieced together my gangly limbs and my high-pitched voice and my would-be-poet's heart and called it a masterpiece.

I don't know why I'm gay, and I'm okay with that.

Maybe we don't need to have all the answers. Maybe even if God gave us the answers, we wouldn't understand them. Maybe we're like infants being vaccinated, caught in a suffering too complex for our limited categories, and no amount of patient parental explanation could make us understand the reason behind our pain.

"Now I know in part," said the apostle Paul (1 Corinthians 13:12), and he didn't seem bothered to admit the partiality of his knowledge. He knew that when human beings look at the sky through a clouded glass and demand to know the weather, all we'll see is clouds, and all we'll forecast is rain. He knew the danger of demanding answers God never meant to give.

Evangelicals are good at demanding answers from God. Is homosexuality the result of nature or nurture? Is there really such a thing as a gay orientation, or are the binary categories of "gay" and "straight" just cultural inventions? So many of the Christians I know and love are quick to ask these questions, and even quicker to believe they've found the answers. They always want to prove that gay attractions are nongenetic, and therefore avoidable, and therefore solvable. It makes them feel better, I think, to believe that people like me don't have to exist. They want to believe that God's solutions all have fairy-tale endings, that there's no challenge faith can't straighten out.

(Pun intended.)

But the nature-nurture debate offers nothing to someone like me. If you prove to me that God didn't intend to make me gay, it doesn't change the fact that I've tried and prayed and failed to be straight. All it does is make me wonder where I went wrong. It promises a highway to hope and then leaves me condemned when I find myself dodging potholes on a dirt road to nowhere. It proves I'm a freak, a mistake, something even God despises.

In the book of Job, Job's friends all have answers. They can explain his suffering, how it isn't God's fault, how it's punishment for Job's sin. They know the nature-nurture arguments. They have a theology that absolves God of guilt and congratulates the non-sufferers for their righteousness.

Nothing they say gives Job hope or teaches him to suffer well. And God, when he finally speaks, despises their well-meaning answers.

The truest friends I've ever known are the ones who offer me more than answers. The ones who sit in the ashes and allow me to weep and share in my sorrow. The ones who dare to embrace God's riddles with me.

■ ● ■

The first time I discussed my sexuality with a pastor was a Thursday afternoon in March. I was in graduate school in central Pennsylvania at the time, which meant that the month of March was a roulette of sun and snow and rain, of stillness and delicious breeze and subzero wind chill. This particular afternoon was cold but sunny, apologizing for the previous day's snowfall by melting it into a slush underneath my boots.

I went to the church building directly from campus, just after attending a textbook fair for graduate students. The bus took me three quarters of the way, and I walked the last half-mile. My backpack was weighed down with free textbook samples. My stomach was weighed down with free pizza provided by the publishing representatives, who had mastered the art of luring grad students to their events.

I felt heavy as I walked that half-mile. But it was only textbooks and pizza. That was what I told myself.

Before my pastor, there were seven people in the world who knew I was gay—eight, if you counted me. But I'd never planned to come out to any of them. The conversations had always seemed to happen by accident. Someone I trusted would ask me an unwitting, too-honest question, and I would answer it on an impulse. There hadn't been time to get nervous.

This was the first time I had made a careful decision, sent an email, set a date. This time I'd had plenty of time to get nervous.

My email to him had been brief and vague, something about picking his brains for godly wisdom. Every phrase was carefully crafted so that I could still back out if I wanted to. I could conjure up any number of minor challenges and pretend they were the foremost questions on my mind. I wouldn't even be deceiving him—there were plenty of things I wanted his advice on.

But if I didn't come out now, I knew, it would only be harder when I finally did.

I should probably explain that this man was more than just my pastor. He was also one of my favorite people in the world. He and his wife were like family to me, a hybrid between very young parents and much older siblings. I went over to their house for meals and late-night conversations and sweaty games of tag with the kids. They were the kind of people I aspired to be: vibrant, unassuming, aglow with an infectious passion for God and life. The depth of our friendship made the thought of discussing my sexuality seem a little less impossible.

Then again, our friendship also made everything worse. It meant there was more at stake. More to lose.

When I had seen him the previous Sunday at church, he told me he was looking forward to our meeting. "I put it in my calendar as 'Delightful Meeting,'" he said, because I called nearly everything in my life "delightful," and people had started to catch on. "My secretary immediately knew who was coming. Do you want to give me a sneak preview?"

His eight-year-old son was three feet away from us, sketching plans for a physics-defying feat of engineering. I racked my brains for an answer that was truthful but not too truthful.

"I want to share a few biographical details from my life with you," I said finally, "and get your advice about what to do with them."

Biographical details. As I trudged toward the church building, squinting into the sunlight and sweating underneath my coat, I cursed my word choice. What on earth were "biographical details"? Surely he had already figured out that whatever I wanted to talk about had something to do with sex. Either I needed to confess my seedy past to him, or I was wrestling with a porn addiction, or I was gay. But I had no seedy past and no porn addiction, which meant there was only one possible topic for us to talk about. So much for being vague.

So much for my backup plan.

When I got to the church building, he offered me a slice of leftover pizza and a mug of water. But I already had a water bottle in my backpack and three slices of veggie supreme in mid-digestion. "I'm good," I said, worrying that the refusal made me sound too serious, too urgent. He excused himself to use the bathroom before we got started. I couldn't decide if I should sit, or if I should stay standing by feigning interest in something on his wall, or if I needed to take a trip to the bathroom myself.

Eventually he came back in and closed the door, which looked flimsier and less soundproof than usual. He pulled his chair closer to mine, sat back in it, and smiled the easy smile I had come to know so well and to trust so unreservedly. "What's up?" he said.

"Well," I began, and I swallowed for a long time.

And then I told him everything.

He listened calmly, not a hint of shock or aversion or even surprise in his eyes, as if I was telling him about my vacation in Tulsa, not divulging the best-kept secret of my life. He was, I realized, exceptionally good at being come out to. It appeared I wasn't his first gay congregant, or his first gay friend. I guess you can see a freak of nature only so many times before you start to wonder if they're not really freaks of nature at all.

I loved the way he looked at me like I was normal. It felt so good not to be a surprise.

Whenever I paused, he asked questions that kept me talking. "If I ask you anything you don't feel comfortable answering," he said, "just say so. I don't mean to be invasive. But I want to understand."

"Ask me anything you want," I told him. "As of twenty minutes ago, I don't have any secrets left to keep from you."

For an hour and a half, I talked and he listened. There was no interlude to pray me straight, no sermonette on the relevant biblical texts, no conniption at discovering that one of his worship leaders had been leaving gay cooties all over the piano keys. There was only compassion and respect.

"Where does this leave you?" he asked eventually. "What happens next?"

"I guess I'll be single for a while longer," I said, because *for a while longer* sounded better than *until I'm arthritic and impotent and the whole issue is moot.* "Not that God couldn't change me if he wanted to. But he doesn't seem interested in that. Not right now, anyway."

My pastor looked at me over the rim of his mugful of water. "You're saying all this with a smile. Which isn't surprising, in one sense, because you're you. You're"—he paused, smiled—"delightful. But what you're saying sounds really difficult."

"It is," I said quietly.

"Then are you really as happy as you seem to be? Or are you just good at letting people see what they need to see?"

"No," I said, "I'm happy. It's a very complicated kind of happy. But that's what makes it real."

He shook his head. "I want you to know," he said, "how glad I am that we're having this conversation. I don't mean that I'm glad you're going through this. But I've wanted for a long time to believe that someone like you could exist. And now you do."

"Yes," I said. "Though I'm not quite sure why."

"Me neither," he said. "But I don't think it's an accident. Maybe you can help the church think differently about this issue. Maybe you can help me understand it better. I don't know what you'll go on to do. But I know that you are not a mistake."

Not a mistake.

Eventually we emerged from his office, not because we had run out of things to say but because the rest of life beckoned imperiously to us. He gave me a ride home, sparing me the mile-long walk with a backpack full of textbooks. We talked about things that weren't sexuality. How he might go for a swim on his way home. How I was working on an essay about derogatory terms. How his car (affectionately nicknamed Old Rusty by his children) was showing signs of terminal illness. We were doing life together, and life was good.

His words reverberated in my mind: *You are not a mistake.*

It was impossible to look into his eyes, the way they looked back at me, and continue to feel the kind of shame that had clung to me for years. Don't get me wrong, I still felt shame for some things— for my sinful choices, for lusting and fantasizing and flirting with temptation. But not shame for my predispositions. Not shame for my sexual orientation, if indeed there was such a thing. In his eyes, in his words, I found the freedom to stop apologizing for myself. I wondered how God might call me to live if it really was true that I wasn't a mistake.

My gay orientation was broken, yes. But so was every orientation, every human being, every facet of creation. The question wasn't whether I was broken but whether I was willing to let my own unique brokenness tell a story of redemption. I was a bottle at sea with a message inside, carrying words of hope that unfurled as I shattered. My broken pieces were part of the story I was made to tell.

When we reached my apartment complex, he pulled into the handicapped spot that always sat empty, the unofficial turnaround spot. I hefted my backpack and opened the door.

"Thanks for the ride," I said. "And the delightful conversation."

"Anytime," he said. "To both. I'll see you soon."

There was no goodbye. Because goodbye is a finishing word, and nothing was finished. Quite the opposite.

I turned my back on him and started up the path to my apartment. The backpack was lighter than I remembered it. The afternoon sun had sunk low, turning from a glare into a gentle glow. Behind me, Old Rusty's growling engine disappeared into the distance.

INTERLUDE
A SONG FOR THE UNKNOWING

Where can I go from Your presence?
Where can I hide that You don't see?
If I sink into the dark, You fill the shadows
If I soar up to the sun, You fly with me

Oh, the mystery of grace
To know my shattered soul and take its place

Now I see through a clouded glass
Soon I'll see face to face
Feel Your beating heart
Trace Your lovely scars
Soon I will know as I am fully known

You saw my heart as it drifted
You saw my tears as they fell
Every hair upon my head is numbered
By a Maker who does all things well

Oh, the power of the blood
To see all of me and say, "It is good."

—*GREG COLES*

◼5◼

STRANGER INCOGNITO

AS SOON AS SHE STOOD UP TO SPEAK, my heart began beating faster. I'd known her for only fifteen minutes—she had shaken my hand and introduced herself as an out-of-town visitor, bouncing a baby on her slender hip. But even our brief conversation had quickly become a political diatribe. There was no telling what she might say now, with her baby tucked away in the nursery and a whole audience listening to her words.

It was the evening of my twenty-fifth birthday, a month or so after I'd finally worked up the courage to come out to my pastor. We were in the midst of a Sunday-night prayer meeting, thirty-odd people gathered in a back corner of the church's worship hall with two acoustic guitars, a handful of lyric sheets, and an indeterminate number of problems. The pastor had just given an invitation for people to share anything weighing on their hearts before we broke into small groups for prayer. Everyone else with something to share had spoken from the comfort of their seats. But she stood.

It seemed an inauspicious omen.

"I think we need to pray for our nation," she said, as the people around her murmured their agreement, and I held my breath, waiting for the other shoe to drop.

She went on. She told us how she was on a mission to spread the truth about the disgusting gay agenda. She told us how the homosexuals were forcing schools to teach that their behavior was normal, even though the Bible called it an abomination. She told us to pray for the upcoming Supreme Court vote on so-called gay marriage, that the gays would be defeated.

Words like *love* and *Christ* were sprinkled in among the others, giving everything she said a decidedly Christian flavor. And perhaps she really meant those words—perhaps she truly believed that the fire in her voice and the passion of her convictions were the best way of communicating love to world around her. But what I heard in her words, what I saw in her eyes, felt nothing like love.

I sat perfectly still, eyes fixed on a distant nothing. Willing my body to relax. Willing my hands not to be fists.

She wasn't talking about me; at least, she might not have thought so. But she *was* talking about me. I was the unnatural thing, the disgusting thing, the thing that made her hands shake and her lip curl. The "gay agenda" she denounced was what happened when people like me lived in the way that felt most natural to them. If I had taken just a tiny step from my current stance—inhabited a different theology, or no theology at all—I would have stepped up to the end of her pointing finger and her threats of divine wrath.

It wasn't her near-condemnation of me that troubled me most. It was the knowledge that so many people—breathing, hurting, bleeding LGBTQ individuals so much like me—really did stand on the receiving end of her words. Because they didn't know Christ, or because they understood him differently, or because they hadn't yet accepted his dangerous invitation to give up everything for the sake of the cross, the only message they might ever hear from this woman was a message of revulsion. They might see in her—they might think they saw—the closest approximation of Christ they had ever known.

The Christ who embraced outcasts and scribbled in sand and refused to throw stones—her words seemed to leave no room for him. When she talked about Christ, I pictured a man too busy turning over tables to stoop and befriend the marginalized.

As she spoke, my heart pounded, but my face was a stone. When she finished, she sat down with a deep sigh.

Everyone was silent. I disciplined myself to breathe no louder than the rest of them. We waited in a silence that was almost like prayer.

Of the people in the room that night, I'd told only my pastor about my sexual orientation. He was the one running the prayer meeting, which meant it was his job to respond to her, to acknowledge what she had shared and move the conversation forward. Not a job I envied. Not a job I could have done at all that night, with my mouth dry and my tongue turned to chalk.

I don't remember what my pastor said when he finally spoke. It was something vague and diplomatic, affirming the faithfulness of God in the midst of difficulty, neither agreeing nor disagreeing with her words. It was enough to keep the night moving.

It was enough to keep me breathing.

My pastor wasn't looking at me, and it was better that way. Because if he had looked, I would have wondered what he saw. Was I showing anything on my face? Was I giving myself away? Or was I winning the game of impassivity, blending in the way I had done for a decade, a stranger incognito?

"Does anyone else have anything to share before we move to prayer?" asked my pastor. "Anything weighing on your heart?"

No. There was nothing on my heart. Nothing I knew how to say.

When we broke up into groups, I slipped away to use the bathroom, a socially acceptable way to avoid joining a prayer group. I got a drink of water, refilled my water bottle even though it was already two-thirds full. I wandered the length of the hallway, slipped into a side closet full of music equipment, lay flat on the floor in the darkness.

The closet. I smirked at the irony of the location. But even if I'd been in the mood to laugh at the joke, there was no one to share it with.

Happy birthday to me, I sang under my breath. *Happy birthday to me.*

Eventually, once my heart rate had slowed and I was sure there was no danger of getting roped into a prayer group, I wandered back into the worship hall. I found a seat in the middle of the room, where the lights were all turned off and my body cast a long, faint shadow on the empty chairs beside me. I put my head in my hands and prayed without words.

Ten or fifteen minutes later, another good friend came and sat down next to me. "I just want you to know that I've been praying for you," he said.

I played it cool, pretending I had no idea what he was talking about. "Oh?"

"I don't know where you're at," he said hesitantly, "or what you feel comfortable sharing. You don't have to share anything at all. But I can't imagine how hard it must be, to be who you are and do what you do. I just want you to know that I love you, no matter what."

As he stammered, a few tears trickled down his cheeks, and his body began to shake. He was crying. No, not crying—he was weeping, his whole body overthrown by sorrow. He hurt for me, hurt more than I had dared to let myself hurt.

I held my composure for a moment, impassive, the trace of my last smile still lingering on my lips. And then, without warning, the floodgates burst open and we were in each other's arms, both of us sobbing, chest against shaking chest. My tears saturated the shoulder of his T-shirt as his tears saturated the shoulder of mine, until I could feel his sorrow warm and wet against my skin. He held me tightly, the way a friend ought to hold if it's really true that love never lets go.

I didn't know how he knew I was gay. At that moment it didn't matter. All that mattered was that he knew me, that he knew how to hurt with me.

I held onto him like it was the only power left in my body, like I would collapse the second I let go.

■ ▮ ■

The evangelical church is a strange place to be a sexual minority. There are so many different attitudes crammed into a tight space— the person who reviles you, the person whose heart breaks for you, the person ready to cast demons out of you, the person ready to scout out a boyfriend for you—all sitting side by side sharing a Communion cup. There are people scattered across the political spectrum, across the theological spectrum. And then there's you, tiptoeing through the minefield.

It's easier when you're in the closet to befriend all these people equally. You learn to celebrate the good in each of them, to know them beyond their views of sexuality, to forgive the ways they accidentally trample your heart. When they say "gay," you learn to pretend that they're talking about someone else. You learn to speak and think of yourself in the third person.

And besides, what do you call yourself when you're gay and celibate in the church? There's no easy word for it, no label that doesn't confuse people or carry a heavy suitcaseful of connotations.

When you say "gay" in the church context, many Christians assume you mean the active pursuit of gay sex, probably indiscriminately and with a variety of partners. They envision the most promiscuous edge of the LGBTQ community, the archetype by which the rest of us are measured. At the very least, being "gay" means that you've adopted a way of life, a set of behaviors, that you are having sex or intend to have sex at some point in the future.

But when I hear most people outside the walls of the church use the word *gay*, they're talking about an orientation, the nature of a person's attractions, not about a specific sexual act. By this definition, gayness feels like a biographical detail as involuntary as your birth date or your dislike of anchovies. Being gay doesn't mean you're actively having sex, in the same way that being straight doesn't mean you can't be single and committed to sexual abstinence. Yes, most people who identify as gay intend to pursue their orientation through sexual expression, but so do most straight people.

In an attempt to clear up this confusion, evangelicals often use the label "same-sex attraction"—SSA for short—to distinguish sexual inclination from sexual behavior. While well-intentioned, this label is also shackled to weighty connotations. The language of SSA was popularized by the Christian ex-gay movement, which vigorously promoted orientation change as the best hope for gay Christians, even while evidence piled up that such change was extraordinarily rare. By talking in terms of attraction instead of sexual orientation, ex-gay advocates were better equipped to treat homosexuality as a passing phase, a problem that might come and go as readily as a foot cramp.

In the end, the ex-gay movement didn't turn out straight Christians. It turned out people who were confused and disillusioned and still gay, people inured to promises that never seemed to come true. Were they failing God, not wanting to change enough, not believing enough? Or was God failing them? Was he just a sadist, a fairy tale, an opiate for the masses that began with euphoria and ended with a brutal letdown?

The diminishing popularity—and, in some cases, the total collapse—of ex-gay ministries in recent years reflects more than just a changing cultural landscape. It speaks to decades of human casualties, people damaged by the broken promise of change. Many

LGBTQ survivors of ex-gay theology have given up on their faith altogether, choosing to hate God rather than to hate themselves. Others cling to faith with tired, bloodied fingers, like castaways clinging to driftwood in a storm, able to believe in God only in spite of what the church has told them.

I don't mean to disparage everything about ex-gay ministries. I trust they've done some good even in the midst of their incredible damage. And I do believe orientation change is possible, just like I believe in parting seas and multiplying bread and water turned to wine. But it's irresponsible for us to treat miracles like everyday occurrences. If we do, the miracles lose their wonder when they come, and we shatter thousands of fragile hearts as we promise miracles in vain. If the only hope the church can offer to sexual minorities is the hope of orientation change, we have a weak gospel indeed.

Because of this linguistic history, I couldn't help cringing when people referred to my sexual orientation as "same-sex attraction." What I tried not to hear them saying—what I sometimes couldn't help hearing—was "This is just a phase you're going through. Every moment since you hit puberty, the nature of your thoughts, your unremitting and exclusive attraction to men—I understand it better than you do. I know it's mercurial. I know it could all go away if you prayed harder, if you believed more."

It had taken me years to realize that God never promised the orientation change my Christian community was promising. Their replacement of "gay" with "same-sex attracted" made them feel less guilty about the painful road their theology demanded of me, but it did nothing beneficial for me. Despite its efforts to free me, the language of SSA simply left me feeling trapped.

There were other ways of naming me, long circuitous titles like "man committed to celibacy whose sexual attractions are exclusively for other men." I appreciated the clarity of these gestures and the impulse to resist oversimplistic labels. But they made me feel like someone who needed to be euphemized or explained away, like the embarrassing second cousin everyone is apologizing for at the family reunion. These carefully crafted titles reminded me that many of my Christian sisters and brothers would be able to accept my sexual orientation only once they'd been reassured that I was choosing not to act on it.

If they accepted me at all, that is.

The beauty of staying in the closet was that I didn't have to choose which word to use. I didn't have to risk confusing or offending anyone. I didn't have to watch the shock in their eyes, or the pity, or the disgust, as I hung a label around my neck and left them to fill in the blanks.

I called myself "gay" in my own head, because it was the best word I knew to describe the world I occupied. It meant that I shared an important piece of my life story with others in the LGBTQ community, that my experience of sexuality defied the experience the heterosexual majority had trained me to expect. I called myself "gay" because I was tired of euphemizing, tired of being ashamed.

But outside my head, among the people I knew and loved, I called myself nothing at all.

■ ◆ ■

When I worked for the church in upstate New York, that first year after college, one of my many jobs was to curate our church library. For a job with the word *curate* in the title, it was a remarkably unglamorous role. As boxes of books arrived, I would categorize them, print labels for them, paste checkout cards on their inside back covers, and shelve them. Most of what I did could have been done equally well by a trained monkey (or perhaps the monkey would have had better luck getting the labels on the spine neatly). But categorizing meant I needed to know what the books were about, which gave me an excuse to become familiar with vast swaths of Christian nonfiction I might have otherwise ignored.

There were three categories in our library that I kept an eye on with particular interest. "Sexuality" (pronounced "homosexuality") and "Singles" lived side by side, two anemic rows that couldn't fill up an entire shelf even by their combined power. "Men" lived in a shelf and a half at shoulder height, just on your right as you came in the door. There were books I loved and books I despised within each of these categories. But in the end, all three categories taught me the same lesson:

I didn't belong.

Predictably, the books on (homo)sexuality were a bit monochromatic. The books that made it onto our shelves were mostly either defending the traditional theological stance against gay sex or promoting the fluidity of sexuality and the possibility of orientation change. During my tenure, we did bring in a few books that pushed the boundaries of our church community's conservatism on the topic, books calling for a love and empathy that transcended our theological stances. Yet even these books were addressed to straight Christians. They were *about* me, not *for* me. There was nothing in them that taught me how to thrive as a celibate gay person in the church.

"Singles" followed alphabetically after "Sexuality," and it might have seemed like a logical place to look for tips on healthy, God-honoring celibacy. But as any church librarian can tell you, books on singleness are usually books about how to stop being single. Rarely do you find a book about choosing to pursue singleness, about regarding it as a blessing and a calling. In my curatorial quest to categorize everything, I had an awful time trying to distinguish between the "Singles" books and the "Dating" books. They were all about the same things, and they all started with the same assumption: that singleness is a transitory phase, something you endure for a season and then shed like a used-up skin.

Homosexuality and singleness. The two categories I seemed likely to live within for my entire life were the same two categories whose books could teach their members only how to escape.

The one category whose books wanted me to remain a member of its ranks was "Men." Our library's books on the art of Christian manliness invited me to become not less of a man but more of one. The authors had taken the time to understand their male subjects, to consider how a man's unique wiring might bring glory to God.

But these books, as it turned out, weren't about me at all. They were about men who were "manly" in the usual cultural senses, men who loved contact sports and daring adventures and female bodies. The authors talked as if every boy had grown up wrestling and burping the alphabet backwards. They offered up definitions of Christian masculinity—our God-given nature and desires and callings—that seemed to have nothing to do with me.

I could have blamed the library crisis on a poor selection of books, I suppose. But what I saw on those shelves simply confirmed what I had already experienced in the church at large. That our men's ministries, our singles ministries, even our conversations about sexuality, weren't meant for someone like me.

I've never attended a men's breakfast at which I didn't feel like an impostor. We'll barely be lined up at the buffet before the men on either side of me have launched into a topic I know nothing about, something like big game hunting or car maintenance. Just moments after I bypass the dappled, greasy sausage links, someone will remark that the abundance of meat on the buffet line proves this is a *men's* event. While we eat our manly meats, the special speaker will instruct us that our families are our greatest calling as men—and if not our families, then our future families, embodied by our fiancées and girlfriends.

For those of us who don't yet have girlfriends to pursue in service of this calling, men's ministries can be supplemented by singles ministries. These are like speed dating services, but with higher success rates and less social stigma. It's fair to recycle the singles ministry curriculum every few years, because anyone who stays in the ministry longer than that has obviously missed the point.

I don't mean to suggest that these ministries have maliciously excluded people like me or to imply that the current state of identity-based ministries in the church is necessarily a bad one. It's inevitable that in catering to the needs of some people, we will bypass the needs of others. If some men are edified by the affirmation of their calling to family and their stereotypically masculine traits, I celebrate that. If some singles feel supported by conversations that regard them as pre-married-people, I won't begrudge them that support.

But sometimes I wish people would tell a story I could fit into.

◾ ◼ ◾

"I just don't understand why anyone who calls themselves a Christian would say that they're gay," said my friend, his eyebrows furrowed in frustration. "How can somebody be a 'gay Christian'? Why would a Christian claim an identity that's based on sin? I might be especially tempted to tell lies, but that doesn't mean I call myself a liar. My sin isn't who I am."

It was a December night in upstate New York, though far warmer than the calendar implied. The Saturday-evening church service had been over for an hour or so, and we were standing next to our cars in the parking lot, having what he thought was a hypothetical conversation.

"I think that's a problematic analogy," I said mildly. "Not to mention kind of offensive."

"It's offensive any time you call someone out on their sin," he objected. "I don't like it when people call me out on my sin. But sin is sin. If we love people, we'll call it out even when it hurts."

"But if you really love someone," I asked, "wouldn't you try to find a way of expressing that love that they would be able to recognize as love? If you don't care how someone else hears the words you're saying, then you're speaking for your own benefit, not for theirs. That doesn't sound like love to me."

"I do care what they hear," he reassured me. "I have gay friends, and I love them. But loving isn't the same as agreeing."

We talked for almost another hour before I finally tore myself away. Talking with him felt like talking with half of the evangelical church all at once. His heart was very much in the right place—he wanted to understand, wanted to love people well—and still his words made my heart ache. I wanted so badly to have the answers that would help him understand—as if once he understood, everyone else would understand too.

Maybe I just need to come out to him, I thought. *Maybe then it would make sense.* But it was getting late, and I still hadn't eaten dinner, and besides, I didn't have the guts to come out. We said our goodbyes. I got into my car, put my hands on the steering wheel, and tried to remember how to drive.

He sent me an email that same night, asking my forgiveness if anything he had said offended me. "I can't imagine a harder struggle in our [church] culture," he wrote. "Any man or woman that struggles with this and puts God first in their life despite their sexual desire is an absolute champion in my mind." He was so kind, so empathic, that I found myself wondering if perhaps he and his wife had guessed the truth about me after all.

Maybe I just need to come out to him, I thought again. *Maybe it's time.* Instead, I convinced myself that the moment had passed. I wrote him back with a simple reassurance that he never needed to fear offending me. As long as I knew that his intent was loving, I said, I would only ever choose to feel love from him.

It was true. But it wasn't the whole truth.

■ ◗ ■

"How would you respond," asked my pastor a few months later, "to the person who says that by calling yourself 'gay,' you're getting too comfortable with temptation? I've heard people argue that Christians shouldn't need labels for sexual identity at all. That our identity should be in Christ alone, and nothing else."

We'd gotten into a kind of unofficial routine, he and I. Every month or two he'd carve out part of an afternoon to chat with me in his office. Sometimes I brought specific questions for him, stories to tell, life crises to work through. Sometimes he had questions for me. And sometimes I just needed to talk with someone I could say anything to, someone who wouldn't have a conniption even if I said something crazy.

"I guess that depends on what we mean by identity," I answered slowly. "I would never want any other identity to alter my identity in Christ. Being gay shouldn't make me into a fundamentally different kind of Christian. But being a Christian also shouldn't mean that I forget every other part of my experience of the world. We have Christians who are male and female, young and old, PhDs and GEDs, Christians of different races and ethnicities and nationalities. Identity labels don't change who we are in Christ, but they do give us important information about how our journeys of faith might look different."

He smiled, a smile that was more lips than eyes—a telltale sign that he was about to make an argument he didn't agree with. "Why do we need any of the labels? Wouldn't it be better if we were all just Christians, with no adjectives? Wouldn't that be more unifying?"

"At the risk of getting all academic on you—" I began.

("Get as academic as you want," he interjected graciously.)

"—I think that historically, when we've ignored differences in identity, people in the majority have tended to ignore the unique needs and challenges of minority identities. We think we're caring for *people*, with no labels—but sometimes we wind up only caring for the people who are easier to care for, the white people and rich people and able-bodied people. I think there's value in naming both the majorities and the minorities, so we can remind ourselves who we might be forgetting."

"So you think," he said, "that it puts people like you at a disadvantage when we refuse the labels *straight* and *gay* and just call everyone *Christian*?"

I nodded. "I'm not saying that avoiding labels is always bad. I don't want to wear the word *gay* like a forehead tattoo and attach it to everything I do. I don't want to be 'the gay grad student' or 'the gay worship leader,' just like you probably don't want me to start calling you 'the straight pastor.' We're more than our sexuality. But there are times I need a word to name my sexuality, and I need a different word to name yours. Without those words, we're glossing over the details that make our stories and challenges unique. When a straight Christian says to a celibate gay Christian, 'Forget labels—we all have to resist sexual temptation,' it feels a bit like a person on a diet telling a diabetic, 'I know what it's like to avoid sugar.'"

"And of course," he observed, "most Christians don't have a problem with the word *straight*. It's just *gay* we don't like."

"Right," I said. "We treat homosexuality like an airborne disease, infectious if we speak its name too loud."

He laughed. "So what if someone agrees that identity labels can be useful, but they still have a problem with *gay*? What if they're concerned that the word has too much cultural baggage, that it might be misunderstood? Why not invent a new label, just to be safe?"

"Because," I said, "most of the English-speaking world is already using *gay* to describe sexual attractions. If I refuse to call myself a gay Christian, if I say that 'gay' and 'Christian' are contradictory identities, a lot of people will hear me saying that they have to be straight to follow Jesus. And I'll do whatever it takes not to communicate that message. I'm willing to risk being misunderstood by the church if it means being understood by the world Jesus died for."

The following Sunday, as I looked out past my piano at the congregation I was about to lead in worship, I wondered how people would react if they knew all the contents of my soul. If I came out as a single gay Christian, would my church still have room for me? Would I still belong?

I wasn't just wondering whether people would tolerate me, whether they'd allow me to fill a seat on Sunday mornings and refrain from flinging used diapers at me. That wasn't what worried me. But would my church still welcome me? Would people still be excited to see me, have me over for dinner, introduce me to all their friends, and gush about how much they loved my piano playing? Would they still take the time to hear my story and go out of their way to learn how they could communicate love to someone like me?

How would they feel about having me as their worship leader? What if I became a Bible study leader, an elder, a preacher, a pastor? Could they let themselves be led by someone like me? Or would every word I spoke, every note I sang, be tainted by my sexuality? Was there something fundamentally wrong with me that disqualified me from leading them? Would my biography distract them from a real, meaningful encounter with God?

If I came out, could I ever again be just the worship leader, the guy who grinned a lot and sang his heart out? Or would I always, at best, be the gay worship leader?

I started singing. I closed my eyes.

Sometimes it's easiest to worship when you can't see what's in front of you.

∎ ▪ ∎

Each summer between my years of grad school, I spent a week at a camp in the Adirondack Mountains, leading worship for a group of two hundred–odd college students. Each spring, as the camp dates drifted dangerously close and I struggled to fit worship preparations into evenings already piled high with dense scholarly texts and ungraded papers, I would find myself wishing I had said no to leading worship that year. But then I would go to camp and watch a roomful of students sold out for Jesus explode in praise, and I would regret nothing.

One year on the Monday night of camp, we had a special worship and prayer night. If worship had been powerful the other nights, it was nothing compared to that night. God's presence felt thick in the air, consuming us, overwhelming us. ("What *happened* last night?" a student later asked our bass player. "Everything just seemed—different.") One of the camp leaders got up and gave a spontaneous call to faith, and I watched as student after student, seven in total, stood and declared their desire to give up everything for the sake of the cross. I prayed into the microphone with words that weren't my own, with a passion that wasn't my own. My team and I played music that was more than music.

This, I thought as we sang, *this is what I was made to do.*

Three hours later, I was getting ready for bed in a cabin full of near-strangers, brushing my teeth alongside a guy I had met just over forty-eight hours ago. "Dude," he said, "*great* worship tonight. It was so powerful. Thanks for letting God use you."

"It was a privilege to be part of it," I answered, right between spitting out my toothpaste and rinsing my mouth. "God never fails to blow me away."

"So what do you do?" he asked, rinsing off his toothbrush. "Is this what you do for a living?"

I laughed. "No, not even close. I've never made a dime leading worship. But I love to do it."

"Well, you have a gift," he said as he shuffled toward his bunk. "I hope you do it a lot more." And without a second thought, he stripped off his shirt and stepped out of his pants before turning back to me. "Good night."

It wasn't that there was anything wrong with him undressing in front of me. By the grace of God, it didn't "lead me astray" or "cause me to stumble" or any of those other nifty catchphrases we work into our modesty PSAs in the evangelical church. But there's no denying that my brain automatically registered the beauty of his body. There's no denying that that moment meant something much different to me than it would have meant to a straight man.

As I lay down in my bunk and stared up at the ceiling, I wondered how my new friend would feel if he knew I was gay. Would it change anything? Would he still be comfortable wearing only boxers around me? If not, would he mind having a worship leader he couldn't also undress in front of? Would he still think I had a gift and hope I did it more often?

And what about the students who had just encountered the presence of God? What about the seven lives newly reborn in Christ? Could they have experienced God in the same way that evening if they had known everything about me? Or was it better for me to remain safe and distant, to let them know only what they needed to know of my story? Could I serve God better in silence than in speech?

If God's calling required me to stay in the closet forever, I believed he would give me strength for that. And if God called me to come out, there would be strength for that too. But either way, how could I possibly decide?

Did the church need another celibate gay man willing to stand boldly and confess the broken wholeness that God offered to people like me? Or did it need another celibate gay man willing to suffer silently in order to love out loud?

I didn't have an answer, and I didn't hear a heavenly voice offering one from the rafters. All I heard was the soft clicking of the ceiling fan, playing percussion to a symphony of snores. The question was still hanging in the air when I finally fell asleep.

6

TO KNOW AS I AM KNOWN

LONELINESS IS A FUNNY KIND OF PAIN. It doesn't require a moment of crisis or an obvious cause. It's a ninja ailment, slipping in unnoticed, strangling you without the courtesy of an explanation. And without an explanation, it's hard to find a remedy. There's no wound to bandage. You can't just wait for the scab to form.

Loneliness never stops bleeding.

After that conversation with my brother in seventh grade, it was ten years before I told anyone else about my sexuality. If you had asked me whether I was lonely during those ten years, I would have told you no—not most of the time. I had healthy family relationships, deep friendships, and more than enough activity to keep me thoroughly entertained. You don't feel so lonely if you throw yourself into the crowd, if you never stop to take a breath.

But the paradox of loneliness is that it lingers inside you even when you're surrounded by people.

I see in retrospect, more than I did at the time, how lonely those ten years really were. All the most difficult questions I asked, I asked alone. I suffered all my deepest sorrows in private, cried my most painful tears in the dark, with only God for company.

I don't regret that season of loneliness. It was, I think, a necessary part of my spiritual growth. Those ten years gave me space to reflect on my experience of sexuality, to see God's hand in the midst of my sorrow, without being tempted to let someone else dictate my story to me. I learned to run to God with my unanswered questions, to look to my faith as my primary source of comfort instead of merely a last resort. I learned that it is possible to have a rich, joyful life even through challenge and heartache—that joy is even more passionate, even more robust, when you realize how much it costs.

What I lacked, in the midst of all those incredible blessings, was a healthy experience of intimacy. I was keenly aware of my emotional isolation. Some nights I let loneliness and self-pity lure me into the false intimacy of pornography. I would hate myself on those nights. My failure made me feel all the more unworthy to be loved or known. And that self-hatred made the longing for intimacy greater, even as it made me more reluctant to come out to the people I loved.

It's strange how easily we underestimate the capacity of the people we love to love us back when we've grown accustomed to living in the dark.

When God created Eve, it wasn't simply because procreation is a two-player game. It was because Adam, even in his perfect, prelapsarian form, wasn't designed to be alone. Sex was introduced as a case study in the necessity of community, the necessity of human-to-human intimacy. We were made to see the face of God in one another.

We need to be known.

In college I was the sort of person who tried to be friends with everyone, and usually (hopefully) the sort of person who succeeded. People knew me as the newspaper editor, or the worship leader, or the guy who never stopped smiling. Once when I told a friend that

I wrestled with low self-esteem, he just laughed. "You?" he said. "That's ridiculous. Everyone loves you. You should have the highest self-esteem of anyone at this school."

People knew me, but that didn't mean they really *knew* me. And it's hard to feel loved when you're convinced that people have only ever loved your effigy, when you're afraid they might love the real thing less, or not at all.

But being loved for almost-you is better than being known and rejected. Or so I told myself, in my rare moments of stillness and solitude, as I suffocated under the ninja pain I couldn't recognize as loneliness.

■ 🌀 ■

The November after I finished college, I found myself sitting in the living room of my apartment in upstate New York, in pitch-black midnight, chatting about life with a friend I'd known for barely more than two months. We had the sort of friendship that could have only happened by God's grace—because apart from our faith, we were opposites in almost every way. He was an Asian raised in America; I was a Caucasian raised in Asia. He was an athlete, a stud, the life of every party, an engineer with a systematic mind. I was clumsy and gangly and introverted and stubbornly unsystematic.

We later discovered that both of us on our first meeting had thought, *I'll never be friends with this guy.*

But circumstances kept driving us together until we couldn't help becoming friends. Before I knew it, he was crashing on my couch almost every Saturday night to make it easier to get to church on Sunday morning. We would stay up late into the night talking, sharing stories, haggling over theology.

He was a master of get-to-know-you questions, especially the Christian variety of get-to-know-you questions. And so I always let him drive the conversation, answering his questions as well as I could and then turning them back to him. After a couple of these chats, he knew things about me, about the way I thought and lived, that only a handful of my closest friends had ever known.

But I was always careful to avoid the issue of sexuality with him. It didn't matter how deep our friendship became, I decided. There were some things that didn't need to be shared. There were some ways in which it was better not to be known.

That particular night started no different from the others. We retired to the living room after dinner, him on the couch, me on a chair dragged in from the kitchen. As we talked, the sunlight disappeared and my friend turned horizontal on the couch. Soon we were just two disembodied voices exchanging dreams and fears and secrets.

"Okay," he said innocently enough, "here's a good one. What's the biggest challenge you've ever had to deal with in your faith? You know, the one thing that could have made you walk away from God, if anything could have?"

I bit my lip, grateful for the darkness to hide my face. "That's a long story."

"We've got time."

He knew I had something in mind, which meant I couldn't stall by saying I needed to think about it. I opened my mouth and left it hanging open in the darkness, saying nothing.

Did I dare? Would I scare him away, lose a friend, if I told the truth? Or would I, perhaps, gain a kind of closeness I hadn't known before?

It was a split-second decision, with no chance to reconsider. I couldn't leave my mouth hanging open forever. So I started to talk.

He didn't say much, and I couldn't see his face. But I could tell by the sound of his voice when he spoke that he wasn't afraid of me, that he didn't hate me. An hour later when we went to bed, he knew everything there was to know about me, and we were still friends.

It was the first time in ten years I had come out to someone. It was one of the most difficult things I had ever done. And somehow, paradoxically, it was also one of the most euphoric. Because it turned out that what I wanted most of all was to be known—no matter how great the risk, no matter how complicated the truth.

I fell asleep smiling that night. Sometimes it's easier to recognize loneliness by its dwindling silhouette as you feel it departing.

■ ◼ ■

My favorite online dictionary has a search bar bearing the default phrase "I'm searching for . . ." So when I went online a few days ago to look up the etymology of the word *intimacy*, I found myself brazenly declaring to my web browser, "I'm searching for . . . intimacy."

As I hit enter, Johnny Lee's song about lookin' for love in all the wrong places came to mind. The online dictionary, bless its HTML-coded heart and its five hundred thousand reliable entries, didn't do much to satisfy my deepest longings.

The search for intimacy is central to our identity as human beings. And yet our pursuit of it so often feels perfunctory, no more thought through than if we'd typed it into our dictionary search bar, hit enter, and prayed for the best. We assume that intimacy will come as a byproduct of more tangible things: friendship, family, sex. When we find it in those things, we thrive—and when we don't find it, we glut ourselves on the very things that have failed us, pouring water into our porous souls and wondering why we stay empty.

The decision to live as a celibate gay Christian is a weighty one in part because it means rejecting society's most obvious pathways to intimacy. The vision of familial intimacy so celebrated in the evangelical church, the vision of sexual intimacy between spouses—

these aren't available to someone like me. I'm left in many ways to fend for myself, to piece together a patchwork quilt of intimacy by relying on friendship alone.

But even friendship can feel like a Catch-22 when you're gay in the church. The fear of damaging your friendships, or of changing them irreparably, can make you hold your tongue about your sexuality. And yet as long as you hide yourself away from everyone, you'll never feel truly known. You'll always fall short of the kind of intimacy you long for.

The human impulse to get naked with another human being is certainly sexual in nature, but it's also so much more than sexual. It's about having every facet of yourself known, every crack and curve. It's about having nothing left to hide. As a closeted gay person, you risk losing both kinds of nakedness at once, denying yourself emotional intimacy in the same breath that you deny sexual intimacy.

Living without sex is difficult. Living without intimacy is a death sentence.

■ ● ■

I've lost count now of how many times over the years I've come out to friends and family members. But it never gets any easier. I stammer, say everything poorly, forget important details and include meaningless ones. Despite what my third-grade soccer coach promised, practice does not necessarily make perfect. (Incidentally, my soccer skills are also a testament to the failure of this aphorism.)

For me, the strangest part of coming out is the demand it places on the people I confide in. It has always seemed brutally unfair to unload my burden onto others, to drag them against their will into an intimate confidence. I've always feared being the oversharer, like the guy in your small group who gives gruesome details about his foot fungus or his erectile dysfunction. I'm afraid of telling people information they neither needed nor wanted to hear. And sadly, there's no way of checking in advance to see whether people want to be privy to your secret. ("Let's say, hypothetically, if I were gay, would you want me to tell you?") You can only take a wild guess and then hope for the best when you open your mouth.

Sometimes, of course, people will ask you questions that make it almost impossible not to come out to them. But even those questions usually aren't meant to inspire such intimate self-disclosure. Coming out as gay every time someone asks your thoughts on homosexuality, or every time someone asks what made your week challenging, is a bit like stripping naked every time someone asks to see your tattoo.

■ ◼ ■

One time I was deep in the redneck territory of upstate New York, walking down a deserted road with an old friend. "Do you ever feel like you're falling apart?" he asked me. "Do you doubt whether God could love you? Or is your life really as awesome and put-together as it seems?"

I sighed, offered up a quick prayer. "Maybe it's time I told you a story," I said.

Just then, a car roaring down the road slowed and pulled up next to us. The driver leaned across his seat and yelled something I couldn't hear. Then he was off again, loose gravel spewing from behind his tires.

"What did he say?" I asked.

"Nothing," said my friend, looking embarrassed at the kind of people he shared a town with. "I think he called us homosexuals."

"I'm glad he took the trouble to slow down and inform us," I said.

"People are jerks," said my friend. "Now what was that story you wanted to tell?"

"Unfortunately," I said, "the guy in the car stole my thunder . . ."

■ ◗ ■

Another time I was at my best friend's bachelor party when the topic of homosexuality came up. *Bachelor party* is a very loose term for our festivities—it was just three of us, him and his older brother and me, eating burgers at a New York restaurant decorated with rustic-looking farm implements and populated by hipsters in flannel. We hadn't seen each other in almost a year, and we were catching up on life, reminiscing about our childhood in Indonesia, exchanging stories from the intervening years.

It was his brother who brought up homosexuality first. Like me, he had attended a Christian college, and he made a few comments about the changing dialogue on LGBTQ issues there. It was a fascinating issue, he said. More complex than the evangelical church tended to let on. I agreed and added a few thoughts of my own.

"It sounds like you've done a lot of research on this," said the older brother admiringly.

I nodded. "It's a topic I try to stay informed on."

My best friend, who hadn't been saying much, looked up from his burger, sincerity and curiosity written across his face. "Why this issue in particular? Is there anything that makes it important to you?"

It wasn't that I minded the thought of coming out to them. In fact, I had been hoping that I would have an opportunity sometime to invite my best friend into that part of my story. But two days before his wedding, at the closest thing to a bachelor party he would ever know, seemed like kind of a bad time.

I was gearing up for a first-class evasive answer when his older brother interjected. "Basically, what he's asking is, are you coming out to us right now?"

We all laughed, me loudest of all. But then, much too soon for safety, I lost the will to laugh, like a garden hose with a kink in the line. I tried to eke out one last guffaw, but it didn't sound like a laugh at all. They heard me. They stopped laughing. They stared at me.

I stared back at them. *Say something*, I willed myself. *Say anything at all.*

We breathed.

"This is kind of a bad time to have this conversation," I said finally. With an opening line like that, there's no going back.

"I'm really sorry," I said an hour later, choking down the last bites of a now-cold burger before we left the restaurant. "I wasn't supposed to take over this conversation. My sexuality isn't exactly a bachelor-party-appropriate topic. We were supposed to be talking about the almost-married man."

"Don't apologize," said my best friend. "Honestly, it's kind of a relief to be talking about someone else right now. Besides, I'm glad you told us. I'm glad you trusted us."

"Me too," I said.

No, coming out never gets any easier, no matter how many times I do it. But my heart does get a little lighter every time. I feel a little less damaged, a little less afraid, a little less lonely. With every pair of eyes that gazes deep into my soul and continues to look at me with love, the thought of remaining single for life becomes a bit less impossible.

■ ● ■

"Now I know in part; then I shall know fully, even as I am fully known." In 1 Corinthians 13, Paul makes this promise to himself and his readers in Corinth. It's his way of coping with the unknown, the unanswered, the mysteries of God. Paul, too, had thorns in his flesh, fracture lines on his heart, reasons to shake his fist at the sky. Paul, too, needed a promise stronger than a lifetime of uncertainty.

It's a two-part promise, really. First of all, that the answers do exist, that they're coming someday. That a perfect God has numbered every hair on our heads and declared us part of his very good creation. It's a promise that we'll know.

But second, and maybe more important, it's a promise for the meantime, in the midst of the unknowing. It's a promise that we are fully seen, fully known, fully loved. Our limitations don't limit heaven. As Hamlet tells us, "There are more things in heaven and earth, Horatio, than are dreamt of in your philosophy." The partiality of our knowledge is no threat to the sovereignty of God.

When I allow myself to be known—when I tell the most baffling parts of my story to trusted friends and encounter their unconditional love in return—I begin to understand the love of God. A love that knows me fully. A love that, when I feel too weak to hold on to it, is strong enough to hold me instead.

7

NATURE ABHORS A VACUUM

I HAVE A STUFFED ELEPHANT NAMED SID. Sid is his nickname, actually, short for Proboscidea, which in scientific classification is the order that the elephant family belongs to. (I don't remember much from high school biology, but this one stayed with me for some reason.) Sid was a gift from a college friend when I spent a few days in the hospital during my senior year. He lives on top of one of my bookshelves right now—Sid, I mean, not the college friend—but you'd better believe that the next time I'm laid up in the hospital, Sid will have the seat of honor by my IV pole.

There are two reasons I think about elephants these days. One is when I'm thinking about Sid. The other is when people tell me not to think about elephants.

It's not that I'm trying to be contentious. It's just that moments after elephants are prohibited, I suddenly find myself remembering what fascinating creatures elephants are. I remember that time in high school when an elephant sneezed on my older brother at the Bandung Zoo, drenching him in generous gobs of elephant phlegm. I remember going on the seventh-grade science trip to the island of Sumatra and riding an elephant bareback, the way her huge backbone shifted wildly under my clenched buttocks, the way I clung to her rubbery, prickly hide trying to stay aboard.

If you don't want me to think about elephants, you can't just tell me not to. You have to tell me something to think about instead. You have to give me something better than elephants.

The psychologists call this phenomenon "ironic process theory." The physicists tell us that nature abhors a vacuum. Either way, the end game is the same: leave an empty space, and it's bound to get filled by something, even if that something is the very thing you meant to banish.

When we think about celibacy in the evangelical church, especially gay celibacy, it's so easy to think about it in terms of the prohibition, the denial, the absence, the "no." But as the celibate lesbian writer Eve Tushnet so rightly says, "You can't have a vocation of No."

I can't measure my calling by the things I avoid. I can't spend my life pursuing a vacuum. I need a positive calling, something to chase. I need a dream that can belong only to me, not just a secondhand dream that might come true in spite of me.

■ ◼ ■

We were walking along the edge of a river in the summer heat, swatting mosquitoes and kicking at bits of decaying bark, when my friend said, "Can I tell you a secret?"

"Be my guest," I answered. "You already know all my secrets."

He nodded. "I guess that's why I feel like I can talk to you. I've never told this to anyone else. But I have to tell someone."

And then he told me that his sex life as a married man hadn't been that magical thing his evangelical upbringing had led him to expect. He couldn't get aroused when he was with his wife, couldn't perform sexually. She wondered why his body wasn't responding to hers. Was he not attracted to her, she asked? Was he spending his sex drive on pornography? He was equally baffled. They prayed and prayed, but nothing changed. Their dreams of having children sat on the shelf collecting dust while they waited for their sex lives to begin.

I nodded and hummed sympathetically, turning away from his anxious face to watch the rippling water. I could think of nothing to say in return. I wasn't the right person to tell these sorts of things to. I wasn't a brilliant counselor or a great prayer warrior or even a married man. I'd never had sex. Going to your celibate gay friend for sex advice is like asking your vegan friend for turkey-carving tips.

My only qualification was that I, too, had secrets I rarely told. I had sexual questions I was still waiting for God to answer.

My friend fell silent, and we walked side by side. I opened my mouth and closed it again, put an arm around him, let the river speak for me. I imagined the words I had always wished someone would say to me about my sexuality. And when I opened my mouth again, those were the words I tried to say to him:

"I love you. Everything I learn about you makes me love you more, not less, because I'd rather love the real you than the person I think you are. I admire you, I respect you, and there's no part of your biography that could keep my face from lighting up with joy when I see you. I don't have any easy answers for you. All I can promise you are my prayers and my love. And you have them both, now and always."

We prayed together. We embraced. The river was still burbling songs of comfort when we parted ways.

A few months later, I joined him and his wife for a late-night dinner. She had a rounded belly and an uncommon appetite and a glass devoid of alcohol. Both of them had beaming smiles.

"When did it happen?" I demanded, which is the sort of question you're not supposed to ask people. Then again, once you've covered sexual orientation and impotence, conception hardly seems like a scandalous topic.

"Fast," they said. "We're not sure exactly when. But it wasn't long after he told you. Telling you gave him the boldness to tell his dad, and they had a really powerful time of prayer together. And after that, everything changed. We, uh . . . well, you know, it was good. The conception can't have been more than a few days later. Maybe even that first night."

"Attaboy," I said, which was probably the closest I've ever come to complimenting a man on his sexual performance.

"We're so grateful," they said, "that you were so honest with us that we felt like we could be honest with you too. It was a game-changer. It means a lot, being known by someone."

"Yes," I said. "It does."

When I met their firstborn child a few months after that, I thought about the stories that brought that tiny infant into the world. In those bright eyes and curling fingers and quizzical smile, I saw the power of the stories we tell, how one person's machete-hewn journey through the briars can become someone else's highway to hope. I found myself believing that, as long as it continues to be told, no story is ever wasted.

■ ■ ■

When most LGBTQ folks hear a story like mine, they consider it a tragedy. As they understand it, my misguided sense of sexual ethics has sentenced me to a life without love. If God is love, and yet my theology forces me into lovelessness, surely something is amiss.

I sympathize with this point of view, because I agree with much of it. God—the real God, the loving God—would never call someone to a life without love. If this is the call we receive, then we've known the wrong God, or we've misunderstood him.

But there's a difference between love and sex. Which means there's also a difference between a life of singleness and a life without love.

I've known love. I've known it in the friends who sit with me over cheap pizza and overpriced salad late into the night, listening to my story. I've known it in the families that adopt me at Christmastime, the steaming mugs of hot buttered rum, the children who shake me awake crying, "It's Christmas!" as I lie with the covers over my head, pretending to still be asleep. I've known it in the moments of silence and long solitary walks as the presence of God surrounds me like a vapor, filling my lungs, racing through my veins, throbbing in my heart. I've known love so extravagant that it makes me sad for those whose whole experience of well-being is tangled up in the vicissitudes of romance.

There is a kind of love that I've forsworn, and it's a real denial, a painful one. But I've received a hundred kinds of love in its place. It seems selfish asking for pity when I'm so unspeakably rich.

■ ◼ ▫

A month or so after one of my brothers got married, I spent a few summer days living with him and his new bride in western New York. They lived in an adorable upstairs apartment, the kind of apartment that fits the stacked washer and dryer into the kitchen, just to the right of the refrigerator. (Which might be convenient if a person were in the habit of storing his or her dirty underclothes in the cheese drawer.) I slept on the couch in the living room, head propped on one armrest, feet dangling past the other.

One morning my brother was already in the living room when I woke up, sitting in the rocking chair, reading his Bible by lamplight. I sat up.

"Were you dreaming about something really smart?" he asked.

"I never remember my dreams unless I'm feverish," I said. "Why?"

"You had your fingers on your chin, like you were stroking an imaginary beard, thinking deep thoughts. Look, I took a picture of you."

Sure enough, he had.

"That's not creepy at all," I said lightly.

"If you ever want to get married, you'll have to get used to someone watching you sleep."

"Add that to my list of reasons for celibacy. How is married life, anyway?"

He thought about it for a moment. "It's incredible," he said. "But it's weird. You have to do everything differently: eating, sleeping, working, hanging out. Sometimes it's hard just to find a quiet moment to be with God."

"Don't let me interrupt yours, then," I said, getting out my own Bible. We sat in silence and read side by side.

I was systematically working my way through the New Testament at the time, and I happened to be in 1 Corinthians that day. 1 Corinthians 7, to be precise: some of Paul's most extensive thoughts on marriage. The opportunity was too good to pass up.

"I'd like to share a passage with you," I said abruptly, breaking the silence. "Some devotional thoughts for the newly married man."

And then I read: "An unmarried man is concerned about the Lord's affairs—how he can please the Lord. But a married man is concerned about the affairs of this world—how he can please his wife—and his interests are divided. . . . So then, he who marries . . . does right, but he who does not marry . . . does better" (vv. 32-34, 38).

My brother smirked. I gave him my most lugubrious smile in return. "Amen," I said.

Before you start thinking that I'm a heartless antiromantic (and a terrible brother), let me reassure you that I think marriage is great. And I'm not just saying that—I have the credentials to prove it. I've played piano for seventeen weddings, been in six bridal parties, baked two wedding cakes. When my former college roommate married my former college girlfriend, I spent hours hanging burlap and tulle and Christmas lights around the reception hall before donning my groomsman's suit and watching two of my favorite people in the world become one. (Who says exes can't be friends?)

So yes, marriage is a wonderful thing. There are plenty of other passages in the Bible, even other verses in 1 Corinthians 7, that say as much. As I'd told my brother more than once in the months leading up to his wedding, I believe marriage is a unique and beautiful calling, equipping you to do things you never could have done as a single person.

But I also believe the same can be said for singleness. There are things single people can do, ways we can show love, that married couples have to forgo.

If the whole body were an eye, where would the sense of smell be?

As evangelicals, we tend to be pretty good at affirming the blessing and calling of marriage. But we're so good at this affirmation that we sometimes make singleness sound like an inferior calling, or perhaps no calling at all. We have 1 Corinthians 13 read at our weddings as if to assert that the best and truest kind of love, the greatest thing we can aspire to as Christ-followers, exists in marriage. No one ever seems to want 1 Corinthians 7 read at their wedding.

▨ ▩ ▨

When people talk about the blessings of singleness, they're usually talking about free time or financial flexibility or geographic mobility. "You can go anywhere, do crazy things, live on a shoestring budget if you want to," married folks tell me, "and you can get away with it because you don't have kids." They shake their heads, a bit of longing in their eyes, and finish with an ominous benediction: "Enjoy it while it lasts."

I'll admit that the freedom of singleness, in all its forms, is a wonderful thing. I savor it. It allows me to do things for God that I might never do otherwise. I can give my evenings to leading Bible studies and running music rehearsals. I can volunteer weeks of my life to Vacation Bible School programs or discipleship conferences. I can sit for hours in the silence of my empty apartment, listening for God's creative voice, trying to write something that I believe needs to be said. I can live a life that if I were married might be only a daydream or a nightmare.

But I need for celibacy to be more than the sum of those things.

Someday I might have to slow down. I might wind up in a hospital or lose my singing voice or get a bad knee that makes travel difficult. I might be stripped of all the activities that define my "freedom" as a single person.

When that day comes, I need to believe that celibacy will still be a calling worth pursuing.

What if, in the end, celibacy is all about love? What if the gift of celibacy is a gift of loving well, loving differently, loving in ways that are outside the purview of the married life?

So often we in the evangelical church live as if the married folks have the corner on love. We pretend that the command of 1 Corinthians 13 is in some way uniquely true or uniquely important for heterosexual couples. We forget that when Paul spoke of "love" in those verses, he had in mind something far too capacious to be contained within marriage.

Certainly there are good and beautiful ways of loving that I will never know because I am single, because I am gay. But I have to believe that 1 Corinthians 13 was still written for me. I have to believe that my life was still written—written purposefully, uniquely, precisely—to tell the story of love.

■ ▧ ▪

"It's just so handy that you're gay," said my sister-in-law once. We were on the highway near the Maryland-Virginia border, four hours into a seven-hour drive, sustained by good conversation and a variety of snacks covered in artificial cheese powder. She already knew that she could say whatever she wanted—that there was no thought in her mind that could offend me—but she looked at me apologetically anyway.

I laughed.

"I mean," she went on, "I have to be careful about being close to other men now that I'm married. But it's different with you. I know that nothing will happen between us, because, well . . ."

"Because I don't swing that way?" I offered.

It was her turn to laugh. "Even this car ride," she said. "I probably wouldn't feel like it was a good idea to be in a car alone with a straight guy for hours on end. But with you, it feels safe. And that makes me happy."

It made me happy too, I realized as she spoke. I loved being safe around her, around other dear female friends who were married or dating or affianced. I could love these women, as the apostle Paul had commanded, like they were my sisters or mothers, without even the slightest temptation to violate that relationship. My gay body knows by instinct what so many straight men must fight to learn: that a woman's body should never be just an object of male sexuality.

■ ▧ ▪

If I can love women differently because I am gay, what about loving men? If my sexuality gives me an advantage in building nonsexual relationships with women, does it disadvantage me in my relationships with other guys?

I used to be mortally afraid of this thing I called "falling in love." As I imagined it, as I dreaded it, I would meet a guy who was goodhearted and good-looking. We would slowly become friends, and then close friends, and then closer friends. We would share secrets. My heart would feel more whole when I was with him. When we were apart, I would think about him.

That, I thought, was love. That was doomsday.

And then it happened. I met a guy. Great personality. Great eyes. Great smile. Cue script.

At first a mutual friend put us in touch by email. His emails were always peppered with smiley faces and exclamation points, his digital enthusiasm putting me to shame. When we met, it was the same. He lived like the world was made of chocolate. He loved everyone, and everyone loved him back because there was nothing not to love.

Sometimes people would compare us to each other, but it wasn't a fair comparison at all. He was my better version, more sincere, more talented, more handsome, more godly. The person I aspired to be. Me 2.0.

We became friends, close friends, closer friends. We shared secrets. My heart felt more whole when I was with him. When we were apart, I thought about him.

I was in love. Doomsday was upon us.

And then, to my surprise, doomsday never came. As our relationship grew stronger and deeper, it became more life-giving. I loved him (in a messy, don't-try-this-at-home-kids kind of way), and he loved me (though rather differently, I assumed), and it was strange and wonderful and at the same time perfectly ordinary. The fact that I was drawn to him in too many ways—that I had to struggle not to make him the object of my fantasies—that made things even more complicated. But it was worth the struggle to love and be loved deeply.

Straight men don't face the struggle I face, and I envy them for that. But they too often miss out on the chance to know other men deeply. The "masculinity" they've learned from society teaches them to hold one another at a distance, to befriend with bravado instead of with sincerity. My gay heart knows by instinct what so many straight men must fight to learn: that men were designed to know one another deeply, to be intimate, to love with a love that isn't afraid of looking unmasculine.

▪ ◼ ▪

One of the most convenient things about being gay and celibate is that you can stop wondering whether or not you're called to marriage. I've watched a number of my straight and single Christian friends agonizing over that question: "Is God calling me to stay single?" They live in limbo, not sure how to feel about the opposite sex, pursuing, avoiding, wanting, fearing. They want to do God's will, which always turns out to be easier said than done when God refuses to stencil an answer onto the wall.

As for me, I've had my fair share of agonizing over God's will, but I'm no longer wrestling with this particular uncertainty. Once you find yourself in the place I've found myself—unconvinced by revisionary theology on homosexuality, unable to conjure even the slightest heterosexual desire, unwilling to marry a woman you can't desire sexually—there's no reason to keep wondering about marriage. Instead you can spend your time figuring out what it means to embrace a calling of celibacy.

And as you figure it out, you can throw yourself into it wholeheartedly, not saving anything for later, holding nothing back.

▪ ◼ ▪

My sister-in-law and I were on another road trip, this time driving north from Pittsburgh after a surprise visit to her brother on his thirtieth birthday. The car snacks lay untouched in the back seat, our stomachs still overloaded with Indian food and ice cream. Heat lightning crackled in the night sky, reminding me to stay awake at the wheel.

Of course, with my sister-in-law steering the conversation, sleep was already out of the question.

"What happens," she asked me, "if you fall in love with someone else in the same position as you, someone who's gay and loves Jesus and wants to stay celibate? What happens if he falls in love with you too?"

"Well," I said, "in one sense, maybe that's ideal. Because as long as I can point to him and say, *There's the guy I would be with, if I could be with someone,* I won't be able to imagine myself with anyone else. But as long as he's committed to celibacy, I'll know he's not really an option either. And if both of us are head over heels in love with Jesus, it'll be a lot harder for both of us to give into temptation at once."

"Okay," she said, as thunder growled overhead. "But what if after you've fallen in love, he changes his mind and decides he wants to get married and have sex with you? Then it's just you resisting temptation. Is that still something you could do? Or would that be enough to make you change your mind?"

I sat in silence for a moment, watching a few maverick raindrops press their blurry thumbprints against our windshield. "Sometimes I fall asleep and dream about a world like that. I dream about a world where I'm madly in love with Jesus and with another guy. At first the other guy and I are pursuing celibacy together, but then we change our minds and get married and have adventures and grow old together. But even in the middle of the dream, I don't quite believe it."

"Why not? Couldn't you do all those things if you wanted to?"

"When I look into the eyes of my imaginary husband, I realize it's not really him I'm in love with. I'm in love with the guy from the beginning of the dream, the guy who's so passionately in love with the Jesus of the Bible that he would rather deny himself for his entire life than risk breaking his Savior's heart. I'm in love with the guy willing to face the costs of celibacy. If he becomes someone else, I become less eager to marry him."

With another rumble, the clouds let themselves loose. I turned the windshield wipers onto their fastest setting. Rain, blur, smear, sight. Rain, blur, smear, sight. Rain again.

"So you're telling me," she said slowly, "that the only people you could ever fall in love with are people you could never be with?"

I nodded. "I think so."

"So when you dream about getting married . . . ?" Her voice trailed off.

"That's all it can be," I said. "A dream. Because at the end of the dream, I always wake up."

■ ● ■

"It was when I was happiest that I longed most," says C. S. Lewis through the voice of Psyche in *Till We Have Faces*. "The greatest thing in all my life has been the longing."

We don't like longing, not in the twenty-first century, not in America. We believe in satisfied appetites. We believe that "the pursuit of happiness" means chasing the thing you want until you have it, until you've gorged yourself on it, until you've realized that what you thought you wanted wasn't really what you wanted at all, until you've found a new object to desire and begun the chase again.

Sometimes we're so busy pursuing the happiness of satisfied appetites that we miss the happiness of longing.

Some appetites were made to persist. Take sex as an example. You don't have sex once and then think, *Ah, I'm all set now.* (Or so people tell me.) The longing of sex was meant to persist. The erotic is by definition something you desire, not something you already have. Sex is beautiful precisely because we long for it, precisely because obtaining it doesn't make us stop wanting it. Our longing for sex is a longing that will only ever find its true fulfillment in something beyond sex.

Lewis again, this time in *Mere Christianity*:

> If I find in myself a desire which no experience in this world can satisfy, the most probable explanation is that I was made for another world. If none of my earthly pleasures satisfy it, that does not prove that the universe is a fraud. Probably earthly pleasures were never meant to satisfy it, but only to arouse it, to suggest the real thing. If that is so, I must take care, on the one hand, never to despise, or be unthankful for, these earthly blessings, and on the other, never to mistake them for the something else of which they are only a kind of copy, or echo, or mirage. I must keep alive in myself the desire for my true country, which I shall not find till after death; I must never let it get snowed under or turned aside; I must make it the main object of life to press on to that country and to help others to do the same.

The calling of gay celibacy is a calling to longing. It's an admission that our deepest sexual desires can wait for another world, for another life, for another kind of fulfillment. But a life of longing isn't a life without happiness. On the contrary, it's a life rich with detail, alive with wonder and beauty. It's when I am happiest that I long most. And someday, when I look into the face of my Savior, I will taste the fulfillment of an intimacy a thousand times sweeter than any pale earthly imitation.

8

QUO VADIS?

IN THE APOCRYPHAL ACTS OF PETER, the apostle Peter is fleeing from persecution in Rome when he sees a vision of Jesus approaching him on the road. "Lord," Peter asks him, "where are you going?" *Domine, quo vadis?*

"To Rome," Jesus answers him, "to be crucified again."

And Peter, who hadn't thought he had the strength to face Rome any longer, turns around and returns to the city where he too would one day be crucified.

Granted, there are lots of weird things in the New Testament apocrypha—like that time in the Gospel of Thomas when Jesus says he'll make Mary Magdalene into a man because "every woman who makes herself male will enter into the kingdom of heaven." (Suspicious soteriology, to say the least.) So I'm not trying to suggest that we should read the Acts of Peter like some paragon of spiritual truth.

But apocryphal or not, this particular story has always resonated with me. I find it fascinating that even though Peter asks his question in the second person—"where are *you* going?"—the question he really wants to ask is a first-person one: "Lord, where am *I* going?" And Jesus' answer becomes Peter's answer as well. "To Rome." If that's where Jesus is headed, that's where Peter is headed too. In the midst of all the things Peter doesn't know, in the midst of his fear and doubt and uncertainty, the one thing he knows for sure is that he wants to follow in the footsteps of his Savior.

Like Peter, I spend much of my life in the not-knowing. I wonder what it really means to follow Christ in this skin I inhabit, as a celibate gay man. I wonder if my experience of sexuality or my calling to celibacy or my understanding of faith will ever change. I wonder what it means to love LGBTQ folks well from within this skin of mine, what it means to love the church well. I wonder what I should say, and how I should say it, and when I should keep silent.

"Lord," I want to ask, "where am I going?"

I'm still waiting for an answer to that question.

But in the end, the question isn't where I'm going. The question is where Jesus is going. *Domine, quo vadis?*

Sometimes I don't get an answer to that question either. Sometimes all I can see is an empty road. But in the moments he does appear, the moments he does speak, I pray I'll have the courage to fall in step behind him no matter where the road leads, no matter how extravagant the cost.

■ ◆ ■

I came out to my parents during a phone call. Some people tell me this is bad coming-out etiquette, right up there on the list of social taboos next to "breaking up via text message" and "announcing your terminal illness on Twitter with a witty meme." But when your parents live on a different continent than you do, you have to get creative.

It was a better conversation than I could have hoped. We laughed a lot. I walked five miles on darkened Pennsylvania sidewalks, draining my phone battery, talking so much that I drank my way through two liters of water. When we finally hung up, there was no lingering tension, nothing unresolved, nothing left unsaid.

And yet there was still so much to say.

The next time I saw them in person, we were gathered at my grandfather's house in Virginia with nine other family members, most of whom still thought I was, to borrow a phrase from my college roommate, "as straight as a two-by-four." There was no chance to talk about sexuality inconspicuously, and we didn't try to. We limited our conversation to boating and music and apple pie baking, and tried to let our eyes say everything else.

A week later, the three of us piled into my car for a seven-hour drive north. It wasn't until we'd said our goodbyes to the rest of the family, rolled up the windows, and added a few miles to the odometer that we finally spoke the word *gay*.

They had lots of questions for me, of course—the good kind of questions, the kind that people who love you ask when they just want to understand. Those questions and their answers carried us across two state borders and into the open grassy hills of Pennsylvania. But I had a question for my parents too, a question I'd been saving since our first phone call, the question that has never stopped plaguing me:

"What if I came out—to everyone?"

I had asked the same question of other trusted friends, and I already had a pros-and-cons list mentally assembled. But my parents' answer to this question mattered especially to me—not only because they might have a special emotional investment in my spiritual and social well-being, but because they had dedicated so much of their lives to telling people about Jesus. For them, as for the pastor of the church where I was leading worship, my decision to stay in the closet or to come out publicly had the power to alter the course of their ministry.

"If you think it's what God wants," they said, "then do it. Don't stay hidden because of us. We're proud of you."

"And what about the people who partner with you in ministry?" I asked. "What if some of them have a problem with it?"

"Why would they have a problem?" My dad was sitting in the back seat, his body shoring up a stack of suitcases beside him. "You love Jesus. You're committed to following him. You're just not straight."

"Exactly," I said.

"Well, if someone has a problem with that, then . . ." His voice trailed off. I glanced at him through the rearview mirror. His eyes were glassy. Or maybe it was just a trick of the sunlight.

Before I go on, I should explain that my dad isn't one for crude language. I've never even heard him use *crap* or *dang* as an expletive, let alone some of the more colorful options. When I was little, I remember hearing the phrase "oh curse and swear" once or twice in the heat of his anger. (Although in his case, perhaps "the luke-warmth of his anger" would be a more appropriate idiom.) Which is why it took me by surprise when he finally recovered his voice and said rather quietly:

"If someone has a problem with that, then screw them."

I've never heard a mild obscenity sound so beautiful.

■ ◼ ■

Domine, quo vadis?

I don't know what's next for me. I don't know if I'll come out or not. Some days I tell myself I'm just waiting a little longer. Waiting until I've come out privately to everyone I love, so that no one is taken by surprise when the word gets out. Waiting until my church is strong enough to handle the inevitable turmoil of having a gay worship leader. Waiting until I'm sure that celibacy is really a path I can walk, not just the impetuous plan of a twenty-six-year-old grad student too young and inexperienced to know the real meaning of loneliness. Waiting until I'm absolutely certain of what I believe, until I've answered every question and resolved every doubt.

But if I wait for that last bit, I know, I'll be waiting until I die. Because there's no sense in rushing the answers. If you insist on answering every question, you're bound to end up with some really terrible answers.

In a sense, the act of writing down this story has been an act of self-discovery, of learning what I believe about myself, of trying to decide once and for all whether my story belongs in the open air.

On the one hand, there's no shame in having secrets. I happen to enjoy the music of Justin Bieber, but this isn't a fact I tend to publicize widely. I don't tell everyone I meet about my medical history or my shaving schedule (once per week, on Thursdays) or my preference of boxers rather than briefs. They're not shameful secrets (except, arguably, the Justin Bieber one), but I don't advertise them either. Why can't homosexuality be the same?

Then again, I also long for a day when being a celibate gay Christian doesn't feel like it needs to be a secret. And maybe if I come out, I can bring that day a little closer. Maybe I can be the role model for someone else that no one could be for me half a lifetime ago.

■ ▮ ■

At the words *role model*, all my warning bells erupt.

I'm not qualified to be a role model. I'm not qualified to be a token gay Christian, living proof that even gay people can reach a theologically conservative conclusion, a test case on which the whole experiment of gay Christian celibacy succeeds or fails.

I'm not larger than life. I'm not a story with a moral.

I'm just a half-written story, untidy and full of tangents, everything up for grabs.

I'm just a human being.

The chapel was smaller than I expected, just six wooden pews on either side of a short aisle. It seemed the whole building had gone on a diet, its sloped rafters peaking high above a slender body, its bare stage and dappled floors devoid of any excess padding. The last of the evening sun sneaked through tall, narrow windows to join the light glowing from a few inert ceiling fans.

In total, a dozen of us had gathered for the inaugural meeting of a new Christian group, a safe space where LGBTQ folks and those who loved them could study the Bible and worship together. As far as I knew, three of the participants openly identified as sexual minorities, and of those three, two also identified as Christians. The rest, it seemed, were friends, loved ones, curious observers, local ministers who had come to listen sympathetically.

And then there was me.

I couldn't have told you for sure why I was there. Not that I didn't have my reasons. If anything, I had too many reasons, all of them tumbling through the spin cycle of my mind, with no telling which of them would be pressed up against the glass at any given moment. So when one of the women in attendance introduced herself and asked what had led me into the chapel that evening, I gave the answer that was easiest to articulate. "I'm here because I love sexual minorities," I said, "and I want to see the church do a better job of loving them too."

The meeting-and-greeting portion of the gathering lasted long enough that I got to deliver the same answer six or seven more times. Each time I was equally cautious to dodge the implied question everyone's eyes seemed to ask next: *Are you on Side A or Side B? In favor of same-sex relationships or against?*

I didn't want to be reduced to a simple yes or no. I wanted a new side, something further along in the alphabet, something full of asterisks and footnotes and caveats. I've never been fluent in the language of binaries.

Meanwhile, as I met people who told me they considered same-sex marriage no different in the eyes of God than opposite-sex marriage, I pondered unspoken questions of my own: *Do these people know the same Jesus I know? Are we siblings in the same faith, disagreeing merely on a single point of theology? Or do they believe in a Jesus who's all smiles and motivational posters, a Jesus who would never dare to demand sacrifice and suffering from his followers? Would they rather know a convenient, therapeutic Jesus than risk standing face to face before the real Jesus?*

But my new friends didn't answer my implied questions any more than I had answered theirs. Maybe they felt the need for asterisks and footnotes and caveats as much as I did.

In lieu of a live band, our time of musical worship was accompanied by Chris Tomlin himself (courtesy of YouTube) as we faced a screen and bellowed along with gusto:

Amazing grace, how sweet the sound
That saved a wretch like me . . .

It was strangely democratizing, standing in a roomful of self-professed wretches and singing about grace. I forgot for a moment to speculate about everyone else's beliefs, forgot to analyze the orthodoxy of the faith journeys of those around me. I was too caught up in my own faith, my own wretchedness, the amazingness of grace in my own life despite my all-too-frequent and all-too-recent failures. Tomlin and his ragtag choir sang on:

My chains are gone, I've been set free
My God, my Savior has ransomed me . . .

The sounds we produced collectively might not have impressed my college music theory professor—the pitch was questionable, and our three-part harmony was shoddy at best. And yet I found my skin tingling, my soul soaring, caught up in a sense of awe. The grace we declared was a grace that could not be erased, could not be cheapened, could not be undone. God would not be thwarted— not by our wrong answers, not even by our unrepentance or dis-belief. Whether the twelve people gathered in that tiny chapel chose to receive God's grace or to reject it, we could never diminish it. Grace would always be grace, and it would always be amazing.

I couldn't have told you with certainty who standing in those austere pews was right or wrong, who loved Jesus or who didn't, who was "saved" or "unsaved." I simply knew that each one of us was equally in need of the grace of God and that his offer of freedom was the same for us all.

■ ▨ ■

One of the dangers of inhabiting a minority identity is that you're prone to being asked to speak for everyone who inhabits that identity. ("How do gay people feel about that?" "What would a black person say?" "Will octogenarians be offended by that?")

These questions are impossible to answer, of course, regardless of who you are. There isn't one gay way of thinking, one black way of thinking, one octogenarian way of thinking. People are people: diverse, erratic, impossible to confine within neatly bounded boxes. Pretending that everyone within a minority identity is identical to the rest is a way of colonizing people, of denying them their right to be uniquely human.

But I, perhaps even more than most gay people, feel unqualified to speak for the LGBTQ community. After all, I'm a minority within this minority. Because I am still closeted, because I have every intention of staying single, I am not a target of discrimination in the same way so many LGBTQ folks have been. I don't know what it's like to be cast out of my family or my church, to be verbally or physically assaulted for my sexuality.

Sometimes when I come out to dear friends, they ask me to help them understand how they can better show love to LGBTQ folks. "Is it possible," they ask me, "to love in a way that people who identify as LGBTQ will recognize as love even if we don't agree theologically? How can I tell people Jesus might be calling them to celibacy, and then go home and have sex with my wife [or husband] and not feel like a hypocrite?"

I wish I had answers to these questions. But I don't. To tell the truth, I'm still asking them for myself.

Right now, my closest LGBTQ friends think of me as a (presumably straight) Christian who talks a lot about Jesus and doesn't waste any time lecturing them on sexual ethics. (After all, if I weren't so obsessed with Jesus, I'd be getting laid too.) But if I come out to them as both gay and celibate, my own sexual ethic becomes impossible to ignore. How can I explain my pursuit of celibacy without seeming to hold contempt for those who don't pursue it?

Worse still, what if my celibacy becomes a means by which other Christians feel justified in condemning noncelibate gay men and lesbian women? What if someone interprets my existence as proof that gay celibacy really isn't as hard as it sounds, and my name becomes another insult in the arsenal of bigotry? What if, by walking my own difficult road, I make everyone else's road more difficult as well?

There are only a few things I know for sure about showing love to gay people, and one of them is this: If you really want to love us, you have to respect us enough to let us make our own decisions. Even if you think we might get it wrong. Even if you're sure we have gotten it wrong. You can't just tell us what to believe and expect us to believe it. That's not how belief works—at least that's not how it worked for me.

I needed to be given the space to read the Bible for myself, to listen to God's voice distinct from all the other voices claiming to speak on his behalf. I needed to give myself permission to hear both yes and no.

Hearing from God isn't hearing at all if we never take the risk of hearing more than one answer.

■ ◼ ■

As I write these words, I can almost hear my theologically conservative friends getting nervous. "But there *is* one answer," I imagine them insisting. "God has already spoken. We can't surrender truth on the altar of whim."

And I agree. There is a best answer to this question. If we love God, we'll do everything we can to find it.

Then again, if we assume we already know the answer, we're not really searching for it at all. We weight the dice, we silence the evidence that threatens to change our minds, and we risk missing the very truth we claim to follow so unreservedly.

Truth is a complicated thing.

Don't get me wrong. I believe there are better and worse answers to most theological questions. Predestination versus free will. Premillennialism versus postmillennialism. Just war versus pacifism. Women in the church. Christianity and politics. We can't all be equally right about these issues. (Though perhaps we can all be equally wrong.)

And yet if I'm honest, there are issues I consider more theologically straightforward than gay marriage that sincere Christians have disagreed on for centuries. Limited atonement? "Once saved, always saved"? Infant baptism? My stance on these issues seems to me so self-evident that I struggle to understand how anyone who claims a biblical faith might disagree with me. But I can't make people read the Bible as I do. I can only explain to them how I've come to believe in the way I do, and love them like Jesus does, and urge them to love Jesus so deeply in return that they're willing to trust whatever answer he gives them. Change of heart, change of mind, change of behavior—those things aren't in my power, nor are they my responsibility. If we can't share pews with people whose understanding of God differs from ours, we'll spend our whole lives worshiping alone.

I say this as a nonpastor, of course. It's different for pastors, for people called to guide a congregation in biblical truth. There's yet another layer of complexity.

(As if there weren't enough layers already.)

But I know this much: the best pastors I've ever had were the ones wise enough to admit when things got complicated.

■ ▮ ■

Let's say I have two female friends. One is a lesbian. She's desperately in love with Jesus, willing to follow the cross no matter where it leads her. After years of study and prayer and reflection, she concludes that God can bless same-sex unions. She marries another woman.

The other friend is straight. As a Christian, she believes that any sex outside of a heterosexual marriage is wrong. But following her own sexual ethic is easier said than done. Year after year, she keeps falling for men she believes are "the one" and going to bed with them. Eventually she finds a steady boyfriend and agrees to move in with him to save money. After they get married, she flirts with cute guys at work to make herself feel desirable. She doesn't want to do any of it, but she can't seem to stop.

Theologically, I am more in agreement with the second friend. But whose life is most honoring to God? Who really loves Jesus more? Who am I more likely to see in heaven?

I don't know.

Part of me believes that no one truly in love with the Jesus of the Bible, no one who trusts the Bible as the inspired and infallible Word of God, could reach a different conclusion than I have about gay marriage. Part of me believes that when my lesbian friend honestly sets aside her own desires and demands and cultural expectations, when she vows to follow Jesus no matter the cost, she'll reach the same conclusions I have reached.

Then again, there are plenty of Christians who disagree with me on other contentious theological questions, shaking their heads at me and saying exactly the same thing.

I don't trust myself to judge the state of someone else's heart. Other people's hearts are none of my business.

"Child," says Aslan to Shasta in *The Horse and His Boy*, "I am telling you your story, not hers. I tell no one any story but his own."

Or, if you prefer the apostle Paul to C. S. Lewis: "Who are you to judge someone else's servant? To their own master, servants stand or fall" (Romans 14:4).

■ ▊ ■

"I used to be so sure I knew things," he said. Even over the phone, I could hear his voice quavering. He sounded tired, afraid. "I was sure I couldn't *really* be gay. And then I was sure I wouldn't stay that way forever. And then, even once I'd resigned myself to being gay, I was still sure God didn't want me to pursue a same-sex relationship. But now that I've started reading both sides of the debate, I don't know what to think about that either."

It was dusk in central Pennsylvania, a hot and humid summer night with just a trace of breeze tugging at the hem of my T-shirt. On the other end of the phone, I knew, it was dusk too. But his horizon, no doubt, was a different shade of gray than mine.

Perhaps every pair of eyes sees the dusk a bit differently.

"You already know what I think," I said. "And you know why I think it. But it's no use believing something because I believe it. That might last you for a couple months, even a couple years—but you can't walk a lifetime of celibacy on the basis of someone else's faith. There's extraordinary value in wrestling through these questions for yourself."

"But it's terrifying," he said.

"I know. But there will be grace on the other side. And in the middle, too."

He fell silent. I watched a troop of middle school boys approaching me on the sidewalk, full of youthful swagger, laughing just a bit too hard at each other's jokes. They were the picture of adolescence: that season of life when you want most fervently to belong, and fear most excruciatingly that you don't.

"Do you ever wonder if you might be wrong?" asked the voice on the other end of the phone.

"Of course," I said. "I'm human. I could be wrong about everything. And that's why I hope you won't take anything I say at face value. Test it for yourself. Weigh it against the Bible. See if it turns out to be made of gold or Silly Putty."

"And what if I decide it's okay to be in a same-sex relationship? What if I get married to another guy?"

"Then I'll still love you. And I hope you'll still love me too. And I'll pray that both of us fall more desperately in love with Jesus, that we keep becoming more willing to give up everything for the sake of the cross."

The middle school contingent split in half to make room for me on the sidewalk as we passed. They looked at me with sidelong glances, as if praying they would turn out much cooler than me when they reached their midtwenties.

"How can you risk it?" said my friend. "How can any of us risk being wrong on something this big?"

"I'm convinced," I said, "that in the end, God is more concerned with the depth and the recklessness of our love for him than he is with our right answers."

Domine, quo vadis?

There are some days when the future feels too weighty to bear. The friends on both sides of the aisle who I'm sure to make angry or to disappoint or to drive away simply by virtue of who I am and what I believe. The fear of staying silent when I should have spoken, or of saying the wrong things when I would have done better to hold my tongue. The loneliness of the passing years as apartment subsides to apartment, holiday to holiday, memory to memory, and there's only ever one name scrawled onto the mailbox.

In Matthew 19 and Mark 10 and Luke 18, the ever-talkative Peter announces to Jesus on behalf of all the disciples, "We have left everything to follow you!" And Jesus answers him, "No one who has left home or brothers or sisters or mother or father or children or fields for me and the gospel will fail to receive a hundred times as much in this present age: homes, brothers, sisters, mothers, children and fields—along with persecutions—and in the age to come eternal life."

Notice that Jesus doesn't deny Peter's claim. ("You've left nothing, fool!") He admits it. The loss is real, the sorrow real. But those things aren't the end of the story. The disciples leave behind the homes and families they know, only to discover that the kingdom of God offers a far richer home, a far more fulfilling family, than any they have lost.

In the economy of Jesus, there is a ledger full of losses that are also gains. The Paul who commanded the Philippians to "rejoice in the Lord always" is the same Paul who wrote, "I have great sorrow and unceasing anguish in my heart" (Romans 9:2). In the economy of Jesus, unbearable heartache and unspeakable bliss join hands and dance together.

This is the dance I have joined, the dance I am joining. I falter over the steps (I never have been much of a dancer), and I lose sight of my dancing partner Joy at times. But she is always there, never more than an arm's reach away from me, a hundred times better and more beautiful and more real than I could have deserved.

■ ● ■

It is Christmas Eve—the first I've spent here in central Pennsylvania. I have no biological family living within two hundred miles. A single stocking, a gift from an elderly couple at my church, hangs from the fire extinguisher in my apartment. I have promised myself I will open the stocking tomorrow morning.

By all rights, I should be lonely. The Christmas Eve service is over, after all—I've sung my dutiful carols and then watched as the dapperly dressed families wandered off one by one to their evenings at home and their family traditions. I have no one to make traditions with. I should be lonely.

But I'm not lonely. I'm the farthest thing from lonely.

There are four of us sitting around the kitchen table: my pastor, his wife, another dear friend, and me. We sent the kids off to bed in their brightly colored pajamas, their eyes alight with promises of Christmas morning just past a field of uncounted sheep.

They give me a basket full of gifts. Lying on top of it is a lumpy green package with my pastor's name crossed out and mine written in its place. "We stole it from his stocking," they say. "He's got plenty in there already. We wanted you to have something to open."

Inside the package is a pair of warm woolen socks. Wigwams, they are called. "Do you have any Wigwams?" my pastor's wife asks.

"Just as of twenty seconds ago," I say.

"They're good socks," she assures me, and I believe her because she's a woman of God.

We open a bottle of wine. We drink (in moderation, of course) and laugh and tell stories as Christmas Eve fades into Christmas morning.

"It's after midnight," someone finally says.

We raise our glasses and toast. "Merry Christmas," we say, because it is.

It's no fairy tale. There are no hands to hold or lips to kiss, no promises for next year and the year after that, no happily ever afters. But this moment has its own kind of beauty. It's stronger, deeper, more alive than any fairy tale I could have dreamed for myself. And it's mine.

POSTLUDE

A LETTER TO MYSELF AT AGE TWELVE

DEAR TWELVE-YEAR-OLD WITH A SECRET,

Everything will be all right.

You know how you think you're going to die at any moment? Well, I hate to spoil the surprise, but you won't. You'll survive long illnesses and bloody emergency-room visits and airplane turbulence so bad you pull out the safety pamphlet and reread the crash landing procedures. You'll survive moving to America and learning how to drive and getting your first paycheck and becoming an "adult" (or figuring out how to fake it). You've got at least one and a half more decades of life to look forward to—and probably a lot longer, if my doctor's optimism at my last checkup is any indicator.

And for you, right now, I know the thought of staying alive that long sounds like a jail sentence.

But trust me when I say that your life—my life—our life—turns out to be something beautiful.

If you saw me now, I doubt you'd even recognize me. I'm the guy you thought you could never be: a guy who's gay and loves Jesus and isn't ashamed to admit either of those things.

I'm the guy who, on a windy Pennsylvania night in the summer of 2015, sat down in front of a blank computer page and began to write. At first I told myself I was just writing a journal entry. (A long journal entry.) (Maybe a lot of long journal entries.) Then it grew into a book I would never publish. A book I would leave in my will to be published posthumously. A book I would publish under a pseudonym, my face and reputation hidden safely behind a steel-plated concrete wall of anonymity.

If I had known, that fateful summer night, where this story would take me, I never would have dared to set my fingers to the keys.

But in the act of writing, as I prodded the past awake and watched my life play back like a TV show rerun, my heart changed. The memories of loneliness, of confusion, of feeling like the only person in the world to walk the road I was walking—they made me wish someone in my life had dared to tell a story like mine. I didn't need an anonymous epistle or a distant idea. I needed a name and a face, a heart that beat and bled and broke in rhythm with my heart.

That's why I'm writing you now. I want to be that name, that face, that beating bleeding heart you need so desperately. (Sorry I'm fourteen years late.)

I know what it feels like to hate the sight of yourself, to hate the thought of yourself. I know what it feels like to be caught between your passion for God and a terrifying new horizon of sexual desire. I've been a misfit just like you. I've grappled with your confusion and wept over your pain. I've been afraid that no one who knew everything about me could love me the same way again.

I see you. I choose to love you.

You have choices too. You can choose to confide in the people you trust, or you can bury your heart in packing peanuts and play the best-acted role of your theatrical career. You can choose whether you'll read the Bible, how you'll read the Bible, whether you'll trust it enough to let it tell you what you don't want to hear. You can decide whether following Jesus is really worth the cost.

Another spoiler: it is.

You'll get it wrong, of course, dozens and hundreds of times. You'll screw up and repent and screw up and repent and discover along the way that God is the God of the destitute, the unlovely, the repeat offenders.

You'll be lonely, but you'll know the deepest kind of love. You won't build a family of your own, but you'll find family everywhere you go. You'll be heartbroken, but you'll be happier than you knew it was possible to be.

Jesus will cost you everything, and he'll be worth so much more than that.

Just hold on. When nothing else makes sense, find a truth that refuses to move and hold on to it. Don't wait to have all the answers before you start learning to live.

It will take you ten years to stop being afraid of that boy in the mirror. But someday you'll see in yourself what I can see in you now: a pristine chaos, a beautiful disaster, a case study in the scandalous grace of God.

I can't tell you every chapter of our story. I haven't read most of them for myself yet. But I've peeked ahead to the end of the book, and I can tell you this much:

It's so worth waiting for.

ACKNOWLEDGMENTS

Stories don't exist in isolation, and this one is no exception. I'm deeply grateful for all the people whose stories have intersected with mine as I've journeyed toward this book—not only because they've made the book possible, but because they've become part of me along the way.

For the anonymous individuals who graciously allowed me to write them into this book, even if they didn't always come out looking like champions. Thank you for belonging in my story. You are champions to me.

For Mike Nappa, my terrific agent and writing guru extraordinaire. "Sooner or later," you once told me (after what felt like our forty-seventh failure), "there'll be a story that pours out of you because you can't keep it in." It turns out you were right. Thanks for taking a risk on me as an author and another risk on the story that finally poured out of me.

For Amy Nappa, who had incorrigible faith that this story was worth telling. Though I only knew you in lovely fragments, what I knew makes me so excited to know you better when we share forever together.

For Cindy Bunch, my preternaturally insightful editor, and the whole fantastic team at IVP. Not only did you believe in this book, but you guided it into an even better version of itself. I feel like I've won the publishing-house lottery.

For Tyler Streckert and Matt Liu, whose thoughtful commentary on the manuscript informed my revisions in more ways than they may realize.

For C. S. Lewis, Madeleine L'Engle, and Nichole Nordeman, heroes I've never met, whose faithful art taught me how to dream, how to weep, and how to fall in love with the divine mystery.

For Wesley Hill, a hero I have met, who wrote the words I needed and then inspired me to find words of my own. Thank you for being brave enough to make me believe that I too could be brave someday.

For my parents. You get the credit for both my spiritual birth and my corporeal one. And as if that weren't enough, you've also been with me through the birth of this book: my first-string editors, my most trusted counselors, and my most faithful groupies. All my best stories begin with you.

For my siblings (both in- and out-of-law), my finest and most persistent tutors in the art of savoring life. It's been a while since our tickle wars, but your fingerprints are still all over my story.

For the Indonesia cousins and aunts and uncles, my Tribe, the people with whom I have always belonged and always will.

For Alvin Dieter Linde, who taught me that life is too short and too precious not to risk everything for Jesus. I'm honored to be your Uncle Keg. Godspeed, you sweet, brave little man.

For my family at the State College Alliance Church and Alliance Christian Fellowship, who have walked beside me as I wandered into dark and unexplored territory. Thank you for loving me faithfully, even when you didn't realize just how much I needed it.

For the many IVCF staff who have anticipated this book with me, especially Jason Gaboury (who started quoting from the manuscript even before the contract was signed) and Carolyn Carney (who called me brave as I shook with fear). Serving alongside you has been an immense privilege.

For all the friends, family, mentors, and teachers, far too many to name, who have taught me to think and speak and love and live more deeply.

And of course, for Aaron and Amy Henning (and their excellent offspring), to whom this book is dedicated, and without whom it could never have been written.